The

Prison Guard's Daughter

The
Prison Guard's
Daughter

My Journey Through the Ashes of Attica

Deanne Quinn Miller

with Gary Craig

DIVERSION
BOOKS

For more information, email
info@diversionbooks.com

Diversion Books

A division of Diversion Publishing Corp.

www.diversionbooks.com

First Diversion Books edition, September 2021

Hardcover ISBN: 978-1-63576-804-6

eBook ISBN: 978-1-63576-806-0

Printed in The United States of America

1 3 5 7 9 10 8 6 4 2

Library of Congress cataloging-in-publication data is available on file

This book is dedicated, in loving memory, to our dad,
so that his grandchildren will always know who Grandpa Billy was.

———

We think about you always
We talk about you still
You have never been forgotten
And you never will
We hold you close within our hearts
And there you'll remain
To walk and guide us through our lives
Until we meet again

Contents

Contents

Foreword

One of nature's gifts is the bond that often forms between a little girl and her father. For five-year-old Deanne Quinn, that gift shattered when inmates rioting at New York State's Attica prison killed a respected and well-liked corrections officer, Bill Quinn. The trauma of his loss fragmented her memory of him. Her mother, trying to deal with her own grief and protect Dee and her two sisters, suppressed information about him. The state, trying to protect itself, suppressed more information. Yet spiritually, Dee's bond with her father never left her as she sought to learn all she could about him and, in the process, about herself.

The outline of the 1971 Attica riot that destroyed Dee's happy home is fairly well-known: the inmates' grievances, their brutal takeover of much of the prison, the days of negotiations through outside "observers," the order of then-Governor Nelson Rockefeller for State Police to storm the prison, the bloodbath when many members of the assault force attacked with their guns killing twenty-nine inmates and ten hostages among the 128 men they shot, and the brutality that state troopers and corrections officers inflicted on hundreds of inmates who had surrendered. Still in need of a proper telling is the account that Dee now gives us of the state's abysmal treatment of the surviving hostages and their families, and their struggle for redress three decades later.

From girlhood onward, Dee sought truth; in midlife she would seek justice. The former effort was not mere curiosity; beset by inner conflicts and immersed in widely believed misinformation, she drove herself to learn all she could about her father, the way he died, the Attica riot, and the men behind the riot. Her search led her improbably to befriend, among others, inmate leaders Richard X. Clark and Frank "Big Black" Smith as well as riot "observers" New York Assemblyman Arthur O. Eve and noted *New York Times* journalist Tom Wicker. As she writes, "My Attica journey was taking me places I never imagined. . . . I will learn all I can, and speak with whomever I can, and my father will one day be whole for me."

Dee's quest for justice was the third such quest that followed the riot. First, a special prosecutor's office (which I joined) sought to hold accountable the inmates and law officers who had committed violent crimes during and after the riot; that effort was designed to look serious yet to fail (moving me to resign in protest). The second quest was a lawsuit by which hundreds of inmates and their next of kin sought civil damages for being wrongfully shot and tortured; in 2000 the state agreed to pay them $8 million and their attorneys $4 million. That $8 million was paltry by prevailing personal injury standards, but according to the inmates' lead counsel, Elizabeth M. "Liz" Fink, "the largest settlement in the history of prison litigation."

The inmates' settlement provoked the third quest for justice, that of the hostages and their families whom the state had sacrificed. In the months and years before the riot, top state officials had kept the prison increasingly more dangerous than necessary. They recaptured the prison in a way that could not have saved the hostages if the inmates had been bent on killing them. Their police shot ten hostages dead and wounded several more. They then swindled survivors and bereaved families out of fair recompense for what they had put them through and thwarted every effort to undo the swindle, leaving widows to raise children in poverty. And they have yet to apologize for anything.

The inmates' settlement angered the hostages and their families—"They started the riot and got all that money."—and brought them together as the Forgotten Victims of Attica with Dee gradually emerging as their leader. The destitute little girl of 1971 became the astute, energetic, and determined woman who, with former hostage Mike Smith, attorney Gary Horton, and many others, sought justice, even though by now they did not have a legal leg to stand on. Four years later, the state agreed to pay them the same $12 million as the inmate settlement. Miracles like New York giving up millions it wasn't legally required to pay don't happen by themselves. Here Dee relates the fascinating story of how she and the others brought it on.

Disclosure: I met Dee shortly after the Forgotten Victims formed themselves and was glad to find her large-minded enough to understand why I had once felt obligated to write an affidavit on behalf of the man convicted of killing her father. She invited me to participate in the Forgotten Victims' campaign as she relates herein, which I was happy to do given the rightness of their cause. As their co-counsel Jonathan Gradess aptly told them, "You were screwed." For many years now, my wife Nancy and I have thought of Dee and her husband David as dear friends whom we see too seldom.

We, the public, depend for our safety on three groups of risk-takers: firefighters, who with rare exceptions are unalloyed heroes; police, who are mostly decent people in my experience but include too many bad apples thanks to too much impunity; and corrections officers, who are mostly out of sight and too often portrayed in fiction and films as nonentities or brutes. But this book immerses us in the actual lives of a group of corrections officers and other prison employees, their wives, their parents, and their children as they seek recognition and justice for what they endured and sacrificed for the state of New York and, by extension, for you and me. I hope that Dee's book goes far toward improving people's perception of these men and women who devote and sometimes lose their lives to serve us.

Of all that I have read about Attica, this book is the most uplifting. Dee shows us in full candor the woman who arose from her childhood tragedy to accomplish the near impossible. There are few happy endings to the stories of Attica. This book has one of them. If Bill Quinn had survived, he would surely be proud of what Dee accomplished. I believe that in whatever Hereafter awaits us, he is very proud of her.

—MALCOLM BELL, former state prosecutor
in the Attica uprising investigation
Randolph Center, Vermont

Prologue

Late 2000. Never had I imagined sitting in a Harlem restaurant, one of the few white patrons here, waiting to meet one of the alleged ringleaders of the violent uprising that forever changed the course of my life. Above the restaurant is a Muslim school for youth. I can hear the students reciting their lessons.

This is a far cry from the largely white community in western New York where I grew up and still live. I have been to New York City before, numerous times, but then as a sightseer or as a high schooler considering the city for college. Now at thirty-five, I'm not here as a tourist. Anything but.

In normal circumstances, I would be interested in the food here. Other diners appear to be enjoying their morning meals. But I am battling a terribly disturbed stomach, a migraine that I'm sure would fell most people, and nerves that I cannot settle.

I am waiting for Richard X. Clark to come through the restaurant door. Known for his "radical" Muslim politics in the early 1970s, Richard Clark was an inmate at the Attica Correctional Facility in September 1971 when the nation's deadliest prison riot exploded.

My father died in that riot, beaten to death by prisoners like Clark.

At least that's how I once would have considered Richard Clark—a prisoner just like all the others at the maximum security prison where my father had worked. In the years after I lost my father—I was then a five-year-old first grader—I did not distinguish between the prisoners. They were all faceless monsters to me, all of them responsible for ripping my family apart. My family would never be the same after the Attica riot, nor would I.

I was not alone in this attitude toward the prisoners. My relatives harbored the same animosity, as did many in my neighborhood. We lived in the community that would be largely connected with the shouts of "Attica, Attica," from Al Pacino in *Dog Day Afternoon*. Yes, Pacino's Hollywood-crafted focus was the prison and the riot's connections to the leftist politics of the 1960s and '70s, but to those who lived there, he might as well have been talking about us directly.

The Attica community where I lived as a child, before we moved in an unsuccessful attempt to escape the memories of what we'd endured and suffered there, would become synonymous with American racism and bigotry. As an adult, I knew this was a simplistic and unfair portrayal. Many corrections officers—my dad among them—had treated inmates with respect before the riot ignited. But that was a more complicated narrative than the black-and-white story told by many in the media and popular culture.

I had personally learned how the simple narrative was often wrong, an empty vessel for the storyteller to shape with his or her own preconceptions. I knew because I had relied on the narrative that the Attica riot—the initial chaotic uprising that killed my father, and the violent retaking by police days later in which thirty-nine people were fatally shot—was the fault of inmates and inmates alone.

By late 2000, I had learned better. And here I was to meet Richard Clark, the man once considered a ringleader of the riot and the man once charged with several dozen criminal counts of kidnapping for the hostage taking during the rebellion.

As I had discovered in the months before my visit to Harlem, Clark was only a ringleader in the sense that he'd gathered up other Muslim prisoners for a security detail that ensured the prison employees taken hostage by inmates were kept safe. He was a peacekeeper, not a riot instigator.

Prologue

I'd also learned that he'd tried to save my father's life.

Throughout my childhood and after, I was told little about my father. I had tried for years to piece together who he was, and I often ran into roadblocks, even within my own family.

What I did know was that Corrections Officer William Quinn was inextricably and forever linked with the Attica riot. He was the riot's first casualty and the only man who died at the hands of prisoners. I could not fully learn of my father if I did not truly learn of the riot.

By the time I sat down in the Harlem restaurant, waiting for the arrival of Clark, I had pushed aside my long-held beliefs about who was to blame for the prisoner revolt at Attica. And I had learned a great deal about my father, though there was still much to understand.

I had decided that men like Clark could help me. And now he has agreed to meet with me and tell me just what he'd done on September 9, 1971 in what was his unsuccessful attempt to save my bloodied and beaten father.

For many, Attica is a lesson in a history book, or it's a television documentary about politics or prison reform, or a fictionalized and sensationalized film. For me, it is far more personal than that. It is the story of my father, of my family, and of me. I cannot separate my identity from the Attica riot, though often in life I have wanted to do just that.

But long before this morning as I wait for Richard Clark to stroll into the restaurant, I had made up my mind: I will learn all I can, and speak with whomever I can, and my father will one day be whole for me.

Richard Clark is one piece of the puzzle, an important piece—and I am here to listen.

CHAPTER ONE

The Prison Whistle

Growing up in the town of Attica, you got used to hearing the prison whistle.

Outsiders might have found the sound alarming, an omen of impending troubles. We knew better. As children of corrections officers, when we heard that whistle, even if miles away, we knew it simply meant that an inmate had walked off the prison farm—an actual farm located on prison grounds, just beyond the high school, where inmates helped raise beef and dairy for prison use.

Only inmates who'd demonstrated good behavior could work on the farm. Our families weren't wary or scared of those prisoners, even when they did try to escape their state-sanctioned punishment. Truthfully, most families in the area thought little to nothing of it. We were accustomed to the farm and the prisoners there. Residents would hear the whistle and assume the inmate would quickly be found. Even if there were a manhunt—and sometimes there was—the families weren't concerned.

As kids, riding in the backseat of our family station wagon, I remember driving by the farm and seeing corrections officers in their uniforms supervising the inmates clad in green. The Attica Correctional Facility was part of our life, woven into the daily fabric for us. A prisoner could walk away from prison, and the nearby residents usually assumed he'd follow the train tracks into Buffalo or Rochester and that he had no plans to hide out in our town.

Attica is a small rural town in western New York, about thirty-five miles east of Buffalo, and the prison was one of its essential job providers. The prison, Westinghouse, the lumber mill, the box factory, the dog food factory, Acme, and a few stores—they were the residents' main sources of employment. It was a tight-knit town where everybody knew everybody; many were related.

I grew up at 11 Windsor Street, built at the turn of the twentieth century, with maybe a dozen other houses on the street. Corrections officers lived in half of them, and their families and ours all played together and walked to school each day. It was a typical small-town childhood—playing on swings, games of Red Rover, What Time is it Mr. Fox. We had a playful black Labrador, Charlie. He and my dad were inseparable.

There was a tranquil reassurance to our routine. We had our cute little house and as children we darted up and down the street most days. We lived without a care or fear as our relatives entered the maximum security prison. It was not unusual for older siblings to be working at the prison, along with uncles and cousins. My grandfather worked at the prison as a civilian meat cutter, and my dad, Bill Quinn, was a corrections officer there. My uncle—my father's brother-in-law—oversaw the prison arsenal, where the firearms for corrections officers were stored.

When my mom and dad first married, Dad worked as an attendant at the West Seneca Developmental center, a facility that oversaw the care of institutionalized people with a range of disabilities. He grew close to the residents, one in particular, raising money from staff for a wig for a teenage girl who suffered from alopecia. She was so fond of my dad that he once took my mother to meet her. She tipped her wig at Mom as if tipping a hat.

My father left that job after a young boy died in his arms after a seizure. That was too much for him; he told my mother he could not return—it was just too painful. He then went to National Fuel Gas, working as a pipefitting apprentice, which he enjoyed. That job kept him in Batavia, close to home. While there, he passed the corrections officer exam and accepted a job in the corrections system, first working at the Green Haven prison near Poughkeepsie, New York, before being transferred to Attica prison.

Built in 1931 for a cost of $9 million—more than $150 million in present-day costs—the Attica prison was then considered a model institution, designed to relieve overcrowding and to be escape-proof. By itself, Attica's mile-and-a-quarter stone wall that enclosed the fifty-five acres of prison grounds amounted to 15 percent of the prison's total cost.

Though in the thick of the Depression, New York State lawmakers believed the prison to be direly needed, regardless of expense. The cramped conditions at prisons across the state, from Sing Sing north of New York City to the Auburn prison west of Syracuse, had fueled an increasing number of riots. Within two years' time, five riots broke out in New York prisons.

In July 1929, nearly 1,600 inmates at the Clinton prison, near the Canadian border, rioted. Police quickly regained control of the prison, killing three inmates. At the Auburn prison in the same year, a prisoner tossed acid onto an officer's face and stole the keys to the prison arsenal. A firefight ensued between inmates and police, with an assistant warden fatally shot.

With more spacious room for housing inmates, Attica was expected to be the future of corrections, billed by the *New York Times* as "a paradise" more likely than other institutions to rehabilitate prisoners. Much of what was proposed—better dining options, more comfortable bedding, more recreation alternatives—never completely materialized, however.

By the time of my childhood, Attica was instead known as the home for some of the state's most dangerous criminals, from street-gang killers to Mafia murderers. The notorious bank robber Willie Sutton, who infamously said he robbed banks simply "because that's where the money is," spent years in the prison and was released when I was four years old. Later, the prison would house serial killer David "Son of Sam" Berkowitz and Mark David Chapman, who silenced John Lennon when he murdered him outside Lennon's Manhattan apartment.

With its gothic appearance, its arched entrances, and its gun towers along thirty-foot-high walls, the prison may have appeared ominous to outsiders, an intimidating fortress. For many of those who lived in the town, it was simply part of the landscape.

Generations of corrections officers lived in Attica. Of course, the terminology when I was a child and my father worked there was "prison guard." In decades since, the term "guard," though still common in popular parlance, gave way to "corrections officer." This change represented changes within the system, as the officers sought to tell the world that they, too, were law enforcement, just like the police, and that they did more than simply keep tight watch over prisoners. Instead, their actions toward and treatment of inmates could help with rehabilitation.

That would come later. What was to happen at Attica when I was a child, on September 9, 1971, would forever alter the image of prisons and what they should and should not be.

I was in Mrs. Lane's first grade class that day when we again heard the familiar prison whistle. What came next was unusual.

The prison whistle was joined by the siren from the Attica Volunteer Fire Department, a different sound altogether, and, though only five years old, I could distinguish between the two. My father was also president of the volunteer fire department, and I knew when that siren sounded, and he was home, he was about to dash out the door.

As we paused and listened in the classroom, neither whistle stopped. They continued blaring. I could not remember a time when the whistles had not stopped.

Our classroom learning came to a halt. The teachers were clearly concerned. They met in the hall, talking about whatever was going on. Typically, the classroom doors were closed during the school day as classes were underway. But this was different. The doors were left open to the hallway, and the whistles kept sounding. Teachers even shut the lights off in the classes, hoping to settle the students, who were beginning to chatter about the strangeness of the moment.

There were many connections between the prison and our school. A number of the teachers were married to corrections officers. Mrs. Krotz and Mrs. Fargo, for example, both had husbands working at the prison. I'm sure those women were among the teachers gathered in the hall, wondering what was happening at the prison.

Later in life I would learn how childhood trauma affects memory, sometimes creating a brick wall that blocks many recollections, other times a sieve that allows some to filter through without rhyme or reason as to which survive and which vanish. There are still long spans of my childhood that I cannot unearth from my memory. Sometimes a partial memory is prompted by a photograph or an anecdote from a family member, but many are gone completely.

Now, even fifty years later, I still see that day in fragments.

At some point during the school day—I don't remember when—the principal came to our classroom door, and I was taken from class and led to the main office. Mrs. Witkowski ("Lowie," as my mother affectionately called her) was there. The Witkowskis lived two houses down from us with three boys. Her husband, Tommy, was a corrections officer as well. I remember thinking, "Mrs. Witkowski, why are you here?"

As the years have passed, I have combined my spotty memories with the few details my family and others shared with me. My mother was at home with my little sister, Christine, who was three years old. My mother received a call from the prison, from someone unknown, telling her that her husband had been injured and was on his way by ambulance to a hospital in nearby Batavia. She then phoned a family friend who took her and my grandmother Quinn—my father's mother—to the hospital. My family had no concept of the magnitude of my father's injuries or of what was happening at the prison.

At school Mrs. Witkowski told me that she would take me and my sister to Grandma and Grandpa's house in Darien. These were my grandparents on my mother's side. I remember riding in the back seat of Mrs. Witkowksi's car. I was sad about leaving school; I had no understanding what was going on.

Darien is only five miles away from Attica, so I'm sure the drive was quick. We were met by my grandmother, Grandma Willard, at the car, and I remember my grandmother saying something to the effect of "Your dad's been hurt at work. That's why your mom's not here. That's why you'll be staying here with us." It wasn't much longer when my uncle Jerry got off the school bus. He is my uncle, but we're only four years apart, raised more like siblings. He recalls being surprised that we were at his house before he was out of school.

I always loved being at Grandma's house; she was a major influence on me as a child and later as an adult. She was a hairdresser by trade and had the most giving heart, and she lived for community service. She loved church hymns and enjoyed reaching for the highest notes. Whenever we were at her house, there was constant baking and she always had craft projects for us—egg carton necklaces, sachets, ornaments made from pinecones.

Grandma had "a pretty room" as she called it, which was my mother's old room as a child. It was all lace curtains and a yellow floral comforter with a small chest of drawers that was full of knickknacks and items we could use for craft making. Although I didn't really grasp why I was at Grandma's, I was happy to be staying overnight. As I grew older, I slept in that "pretty room" plenty of times, always enjoying a sleepover with Grandma.

There are other memories from those days—very few, yet some are vivid.

My grandmother's home was very busy, as I recall, but the memory that is most entrenched is the police surveillance that was there and stayed for days. My uncle Jerry remembers workmen on a pole between my grandparents' home and the next-door neighbor. My grandfather told him they were actually police officers keeping an eye on the house. At times there were as many as six police cars in the driveway.

A door in Grandma's kitchen led to the basement. Once, I heard voices from the basement and opened the door. My grandmother quickly shut it, saying, "That's not a place for young ladies." I saw police downstairs; I'd later learn they were state troopers.

My grandfather was not a man who usually kept a tight eye on us. But while we were staying at his house during the riot, he constantly knew where we were, and, I suspect, so did some of those troopers.

I didn't know that there had been a huge riot at the prison and that the nation was now paying attention to my small town of Attica and the place where my father worked. The prison was always in my periphery, whether we were going to the dump on Saturdays or taking a ride in the country after getting ice cream. Driving by the prison superintendent's mansion and seeing the inmates mowing the lawn was normal. We'd drive by the prison and Dad would tell us that that was where he worked. I remember thinking, "That's where the bad people live."

The State Police were at my grandparents' house because there were fears of retaliation against the families of corrections officers. We were told that buses were coming in from Rochester and Buffalo with protesters. There were rumors that the Black Panthers were coming to Attica to support the inmates. The Black Panthers were considered radical and frightened many people in my community, which was almost all white. The police were at my grandparents' home to keep our family safe. There were worries that the family of William Quinn could be in danger.

Having so many police around must have made an impression on me, because I do remember their presence so clearly. But my memories of the next few days are scattered. Or they're gone altogether.

It must have been my grandmother who told us Dad was hurt badly enough to remain hospitalized and that Mom would be staying at his bedside. I knew they had moved him from the Batavia hospital to a hospital in Rochester. I had an understanding that he was severely injured, but I wasn't aware of the circumstances.

I doubt anyone told us specifically that during the uprising my father had tried to secure a prison gate against inmates charging against it. The gate gave way, and prisoners beat him as he lay on the ground. He suffered two open skull fractures, and his hands and arms were in terrible shape, severely injured as he tried to protect himself from the assault.

I certainly did not know that a fellow officer and even inmates tried to save my father after the beating. Four inmates carried him on a mattress to the administration building and told corrections officials they needed to get him to a hospital. But corrections officials left him on that mattress for almost two hours before finally taking him out of the prison by ambulance. This I would learn much later in life.

Many years later, my sister and I listened to a corrections officer tell how he and some colleagues saw my dad on the bloody mattress, with his hands involuntarily flexing to cover his face, while they stepped over him to clock into the prison to help other corrections officers try to regain control of the housing blocks. I have spent a lot of time wondering if quicker action could have saved my father's life. I'll never know.

My father died on September 11, two days after the outbreak of the riot. On that day, inmates were holding hostages in the prison yard, trying to negotiate a resolution without further violence. Those efforts would fail—terribly. On the morning of September 13, 1971—a dreary, gray day that seemed to portend what was to come—helicopters hovered over the prison, dropping tear gas. Police then stormed the prison, their gunfire killing thirty-nine and injuring more than eighty. Ten prison employee hostages were among the slain. My father was the only prison employee killed at Attica not by police gunfire.

My uncle Jerry remembers the day his sister—my mother—came back home from the hospital after my father died. She cried inconsolably. She told me and Christine about my father's death. We stayed at my grandparents' house for another three weeks; my mother needed support from her parents and our immediate family. During that time my mother consulted our family pastor as to whether or not my sister and I should attend my father's funeral. In the end, we were not allowed to attend; neither did Jerry, although he says the decision was left up to him.

My father's funeral was on September 15, 1971, and he was the first of the prison employee victims to be buried. Calling hours were at Marley's Funeral Home on Main Street followed by a Catholic burial at St. Anthony's, across the street from where my grandparents lived.

There's one photograph, from United Press International, that I first came across as a high school student trying to do my own secretive research into the riot. To this day, that picture sticks with me and I have gone back many times to look at it again: rows and rows of corrections officers and volunteer firefighters, marching in a solemn processional to the cemetery. They are four abreast, and there is a unity and precision in their stride, with dozens of uniformed men advancing through the village of Attica behind the hearse carrying my father to his resting place.

That photo still takes my breath away, even today—so many people at my dad's funeral at a time when many of those same people marching were grieving with their own families. When you see that photograph, it is a statement that Bill Quinn's family is supported by corrections officers, by his fellow firefighters. It is a brotherhood, and it remained that way in the most trying and tragic of times.

I have seen pictures of my mother at the funeral. It breaks my heart. It looks like she's being physically held up by my grandparents. She looks so out of sorts, so lost, so heartbroken.

We moved back to our little house in Attica and I remember we were not allowed to play or even go outside without an adult. Our peacefulness was disrupted, our world askew, our childhood innocence ruptured.

The news media—TV, radio, newspapers—gathered on our street, hoping for interviews. They were feeding on our grief. The neighbors often tried to shoo them away. Both of my grandfathers, as well as family friends, would come to the house to ensure that aggressive reporters stayed off the porches and didn't try to talk to my mother. Our wall phone was taken off the hook because the media kept calling.

Some of my memories are clearly those of a child. As my family worried about my father's condition, and then grieved his death, I was upset that I could not go outside. I had recently gotten a new bike and I was mad that I couldn't ride it up and down the street as I had before with the neighborhood kids. Of course, there were no other kids riding bikes on the street; everyone was in their homes avoiding the media just as we were.

It was at our house in Attica that I finally understood that my dad was never returning home. Again, I only have slivers of memories: my dad's work shirt on the back of a chair; my mom crying often; relatives at the house, especially Grandma Willard.

Aunt Fran, my father's sister, took medication so that she could cope immediately following the riot. Her husband, Bob, the arsenal supervisor, was my father's best friend, and he was devastated. We were all in our own emotional free fall. Back then, there was no one to catch you.

Several weeks after the funeral, my mother was not feeling well. At the doctor's office, she learned she was pregnant and due in May. She was shocked and overwhelmed, and many offered her advice, whether sought after or not, as to what to do. Even the doctor suggested she consider terminating the pregnancy, saying life could be terribly difficult for her with three young children. She told the doctor, "This baby is all I have left of him."

On May 26, 1972, we got our new baby sister, Amy, who looked remarkably like our father. Dark hair, fair skin, dark eyes, and the famous Quinn family pointy chin. Our grandparents were in the hospital waiting room of the Labor and Delivery Ward—my grandfathers were notably the oldest men at the hospital—waiting to catch a glimpse of the newest Quinn baby. It was the first time in a long while that our family had experienced some happiness, especially my mother.

After Amy's birth, the wives of other corrections officers threw a baby shower. Little Amy, sitting in a bouncy chair, joined the festivities. Mom had not wanted a shower before Amy's birth; she later told me she wanted to focus on caring for us girls.

With a new sister and my father gone, we tried to return to life as if it were normal. Of course, it wasn't. But the pediatrician told my mother to have us return to school and to get the kids back on a routine schedule. She was told that would be best for us.

I internalized a lot of the pain. I remember returning to school and trying to pull myself together. I got sick and threw up at my desk multiple times. I was what you'd probably call a sickly child. I had severe stomach problems when young. I suffered from anxiety, which largely went undiagnosed. Today, there is more in place to identity and intervene with children who are struggling. But I had no choice but to find a way to cope on my own, to cope with what we'd lost, to cope with my life at home, which was far from easy.

My memories of my father are limited, perhaps also erased or blurred by my trauma. I distinctly recall walking his beloved Labrador Charlie with him, leading Charlie to the kennel my father built for him in our yard. I recall my dad puttering with his tools in our tiny garage. We did not keep a car in there; it was just too small for a car, but it did fit our bikes.

There was a grate on the first floor of our house that blew heated air from our furnace, and I remember sitting there in that warmth with my sister, Christine, as our father prepared breakfast some mornings. You could also see the television in the living room from the grate, so it was an optimal place for a child to sit.

Beyond that, my memories are few. My mom would sometimes remark that my smile or something I'd said reminded her of Dad, as if she were catching a fleeting glimpse of the husband she'd lost.

My mother had her hands full. She was grieving herself while taking care of two young girls and a newborn. I had many emotions going on. I did not fully grasp the enormity of our loss but did feel the changes within our home. This manifested in my stomach woes.

My illness reminded my mother of whom we'd lost. It reminded her of all the dreams she'd lost with the death of my father. Things were far from fine in our home and would likely never be fine again.

I did not recognize then how much my mother was suffering. She remarried in February 1973. Later that year my mother and stepfather had a child, my half sister. I believe my mother may have thought having a husband, a new stepfather for her children, and a baby would return life to what it once was.

It didn't.

CHAPTER TWO

Struggles at Home

The stomach issues continued for me as a child. My mother and I
returned time after time to the doctor, receiving diagnosis after
diagnosis. Whatever intestinal ailment you can name, I was diagnosed
with it—ulcerative colitis, colitis, abdominal angina, IBS. I'd typically
spend at least one night a week out of my bed and on the couch with my
mother taking care of me, comforting me, trying to help me feel better.

I was prescribed a number of bizarre medications, some of which
were meant for adults. One medication was so overpowering in its
potency that I nearly passed out in the bathtub. Thankfully my mother
was there.

I think my mother suspected the root cause might be anxiety. When
I would get stricken with the stomach aches, we would sit up and talk.
She would ask if anything at school was bothering me, was I having issues
with friends, or whether something else might be weighing on my mind.
My mother would never try to prod me to go back to bed even if I woke
up in the middle of the night. She was always there to listen, regardless
of how exhausted she must have been in a home with four young girls. I
could tell her about nearly anything. Still, we rarely spoke of my father. I

was always hesitant to raise the topic of my dad, and my mother was still dealing with her own pain, so neither of us spoke about it.

I always felt better after we talked, but there was still something constant and underlying that brought on these physical symptoms. I think it was more about the constant questions I had about my father and his death. Even as a kid, I simply felt there was so much I did not know.

I believe the pain also came from change. My mother had remarried and we'd moved to the nearby town of Darien when I was around ten. There were so many changes in a short period of time, and they added to the uncertainty in my life. My mother and new stepfather sold our house on Windsor Street in Attica, and we left my comfortable hometown where my dad's parents also lived. We built a house in Darien to be closer to my mom's parents.

I didn't want to leave Attica, and I let my mother know. She understood that I didn't want to say goodbye to my neighborhood and all my friends, but I knew I had no control over this decision. My parents thought this was a positive move for us—move on and leave Attica behind—but I was simply trying to keep my head above water, physically and emotionally.

I started fifth grade in a new school, had to make new friends, and my entire environment was uprooted in a matter of a few short years. On top of all of the changes was the lingering loss of my father. I was told, of course, that my father was killed, and he was not going to come back. I knew he was never coming home, but my world had been disrupted and I was getting little help as to how to survive. The best thing for me, in my new household, was to just try to adjust and go with the flow. That didn't work so well either.

In my childhood I would sometimes gather up the courage to ask my mom or relatives questions about my father, only to receive small bits of information. I'm still not sure if this was an attempt to shield my sisters and me from the truth or if it was instead a form of my family's own self-preservation. But, after my father's death, his parents rarely spoke about him. My grandparents were strong Irish Catholics, but the death of their son was just too much to bear. I always knew that my questions about my father were sometimes not welcome, bringing back memories too painful for anyone in my family to relive, especially for my mother. I longed to know what my father was like, since my cherished childhood memories continued to fade with each passing day.

When I did ask Mom a question about my dad, I'd try to make sure no one else was around, hoping that this would be the time she'd be agreeable to talking and sharing a story or two about my father. Often her answers were short and never laden with details. I could always tell when additional questions were discouraged. I sometimes felt guilty for asking; her eyes welled with tears at the very mention of my father. I knew she missed him as much as I did, but, as she would say, we needed to "get on with life."

Though we'd moved to Darien, we were still only five miles from Attica. I had new classmates who were the children of corrections officers and many knew of the death of my father. My sisters and I were often asked in school, at the local grocery store, and at community events if we were the children of Billy Quinn, the prison guard killed at Attica. My sister Amy later joked that she was told by our mother on the first day of school, "Have a good day and, by the way, don't be surprised if they ask if you're the daughter of Bill Quinn." It felt like everyone knew more about the death of our father than we did. It was often at school that I found myself exceptionally stricken by my stomach troubles. I knew the school nurse very well, and she, too, knew my family's history.

By the time I reached junior high school, the riot would sometimes be discussed in classes. I first recall the riot coming up in a social studies class. I'm not sure if the rest of the country studied the riot—after all this was only eight years later—but I assume we did because of the proximity to the prison and its history.

The teacher had his eye on me. Imagine the precarious position he was in, discussing Attica with the daughter of a slain corrections officer in the room. There were other kids who were also the children of prison employees.

He was also the football coach, and he looked like a football coach—a huge man with a thick handlebar moustache. Thankfully, he was a kind man, and he could see that I was beginning to grow upset as he talked about the riot. I wondered if he was thinking, "Oh God, I'm trying to teach and I'm looking in the corner and this kid is falling apart on me." He asked me if I wanted to leave class, and I did. I went to the nurse's office again, feeling ill. My stomach pains flared, and I was sent home.

That continued to happen at school. The riot's anniversary would typically prompt discussions, and at other times in the school year it would come up in the normal curriculum flow. I'd get upset because the lessons seemed to contradict what little information I received at home. The histories of Attica did not portray the inmates as monsters. Instead, the histories, limited as they were when I was a teenager, seemed to treat the inmates with more sympathy.

I heard of the conditions at the prison that gave rise to the riot—the prison administration's pushback against religious freedom for inmates, once-a-week showers, one roll of toilet paper a month for the prisoners, and limited educational opportunities. The prison, built forty years before the riot as a "paradise" for inmates—an answer to overcrowded prisons—was itself severely overcrowded at the time of the uprising, housing nearly 2,300 inmates, which was 45% over planned capacity. And there was racial tension. The staff at the prison was almost entirely white, while much of the prison population was Black and Latino. Racism manifested in policies: the mail to Black and Latino inmates was often censored more than other incoming inmate mail, and those prisoners were denied magazines targeted to their communities.

But in my household, what I was told was cut and dry: The inmates, who were awful people, violently rioted and murdered my father. My world was simple: All of the inmates were bad. That was the lesson imparted on the rare occasion when someone in my family discussed the riot. My family was not alone. Many in the community, especially those who had corrections officers in the family, felt the same.

My cousin Michael and I were the same age and in some classes together. He seemed unaffected by the discussions, and he would remain in class. I knew the impact the loss of my father had on Michael's father, my uncle Bob, who was my dad's dearest friend. Bob could not speak of the riot or my father afterward.

Bob's wife, my aunt Fran, was the rare individual who would talk about my father with me when I was young. She told me that he'd been an Eagle Scout and that he loved fishing. But his death was still very difficult for her, as well. I remember being told that a doctor had made a house call in the days after the riot. He brought medications for Aunt Fran and my grandmother on my father's side. I later realized that they were receiving medicines simply to help them survive day by day.

I wasn't told much at home at all about the retaking and the fatal shootings when armed police and corrections officers stormed the prison grounds on September 13, 1971, firing wildly. And, if I did hear anything at all, the retaking was typically framed as justified and necessary, even though civilian hostages were killed as well as prisoners.

When I was older, there were times in school when I did stay for some of the lesson and heard the side of the riot history that challenged the decisions state officials had made to regain control of Attica on September 13. I was convinced it was untrue. It did not mesh with what little I had been told at home through the years.

But I wouldn't stand up and tell the teachers that they were wrong, that their version of the Attica riot was misinformed. Instead, I'd simply get ill again. It got to the point where the teacher in my current events class would tell me in advance when a class was to focus on the riot and would ask if I wanted to leave the classroom. I would then go to the nurse's office or sit in the hallway until the class had moved on to whatever topic was next. My cousin Michael always stayed.

I didn't talk to others in junior high about my father and his murder at Attica, but I sensed that everyone knew who I was and my connection to the riot. And I knew my connection, but I did not know my history. Those are two very different things. Yes, I was the teenage daughter of the first person to die in the Attica riot, but who was I beyond that? I recognized that there was more to know, more to learn, and I could either run from it or search for it.

As a teenager, I'd go to the school library and the public library and look for books on the riot. I'd go into the card catalogue—that's how we found library books in those days—and flip through the cards for the topic of Attica.

I'd often search out the official report on the riot from what was called the McKay Commission, a panel put together by state legislators after the riot to review what happened and what state officials and police could have and should have done differently. The commission was chaired by Robert McKay, the dean of the New York University Law School and a former president of the New York City Bar Association. The state used its own as investigators to investigate itself.

The report was also published as a book, and you could find it in libraries and at stores. On the front page was a photo of naked inmates, lined up on both sides of an armed state trooper, their hands behind their heads. After the retaking of the prison on September 13, the police forced the prisoners to strip naked to be sure they had no homemade weapons on them as the inmates were returned to housing in the prison.

My mother also kept a copy of the McKay Commission in her nightstand—hidden beneath a pile of magazines. To this day, she does not remember having one. She doesn't like to read, and I know she never actually read it. But when she and my stepfather would go out for dinner or be away for some other reason I'd sneak into their room and read it. I'm not sure how I first found it, but I'd wait for them to leave so I could pull out the McKay Commission report.

I'd always go to the index and look up "William Quinn" and find the pages about my father. I would read for as long as I could and hope I would not get caught. I didn't tell anyone that I was reading the McKay; I kept it to myself. But, somehow, the whole experience—trying secretly to learn about my father and the riot—made me more confused.

Once my mother did catch me reading it and I got in trouble. I hadn't heard her return or come into the bedroom; perhaps I was too engrossed in the book. What's funny was that my mother, as I recall, was not disturbed that I might be searching out information about my father in the book. Instead, she wanted to keep me and my sisters away from the picture of the naked inmates on the cover. She didn't want us to see that.

Sometimes I would bring home library books about Attica. But, once I got them home, I was not encouraged to read them. Instead, I was reminded they were likely filled with lies and should not be believed.

In some of my reading I would search out information on John Hill, an Attica inmate convicted in 1975 of murdering my father, and Charles Pernasilice, who was convicted of attempted assault in the fatal beating of my father. I didn't dare mention the names at my house. Little was ever said about them.

Life at home was far from easy. My stepfather and I were not close. There was a strain of racism that ran through him, and this was new to me and my household. I don't recall racism within my home when my father was alive. As I would later discover, my father was respected by many of the inmates at the prison, and some would come to him for advice.

I tiptoed around my stepfather's racism. He, of course, wasn't alone, and he was a product of his time and environment. Others in the community, which was almost entirely white, often felt as he did.

As a teenager, most of my days were spent surviving, in school and at home. I often just wanted to be out of the house. You could stay at school when classes were over and do your homework there and take a later bus home. I typically did that just to keep away from home a little longer.

Beginning in seventh grade, I ran track. It was my outlet, and I loved it. I was a sprinter, and I relished the meets and the opportunity to travel and gather with others from around the region. There was something freeing about it. I ran in both winter and spring track seasons. We were good. We went to our regional sectional meets every year—events for only the top teams—and finished third in the state one year and set a school record in the 4x100 relay.

Some winter meets were held at the University of Rochester, about an hour east of Darien. The university had an indoor track, and teams from across western New York would participate in meets. There were schools of every size there. It was an awesome place to be because of the variety of people. All of my teammates were white, and, in our typical regional meets at other locations, I was running against other rural schools and most everyone was white there, as well. I'd go to the University of Rochester and everybody had their music playing and there were people of all colors. It was a far more diverse environment with an energy unlike other meets. Some kids were playing some funky music, some were playing AC/DC, and we'd dance together and be goofy—typical teenage stuff.

The indoor track at the University of Rochester had a short tunnel you had to run through, and that's where the competitiveness really came out. It was a four-lane, two-hundred-meter track, squeezed in the tunnel, and you're bumping each other for an advantage. If you were worth your weight in salt, you threw an elbow or two in the tunnel. Sometimes you worried people might not come out the other side. I was highly competitive in track and everything else; I still am.

Struggles at Home

At the University of Rochester meets, we'd often pile our gear together, and you'd get to know members from the teams who left their gear alongside yours. One of those teams came from the Bath-Haverling High School, and I talked with them a lot. They were the friendliest people, and they also had great taste in music, which was a plus.

On that team was a teenager named Kory, and we became fast friends. As Kory put it later in life, "When we first met, it was like lightning in a bottle." He was right. He, too, was a sprinter, and we would often talk as we waited for our events. They ran the girls' events before the boys' and we were always at the starting lines together.

Kory, who is Black, had also experienced tragedy in his life.

Kory and his twin brother were placed in foster care as infants. Kory's biological mother specifically requested that the two boys be fostered by the Kraft family, who had a long history in the area of being wonderful loving people. They had four children of their own and fostered others, as well. At the age of five, Kory and his twin were legally adopted into the Kraft family. Mrs. Kraft was a nurse and Mr. Kraft a laboratory scientist.

Kory knew his biological mother and was aware of some of her struggles with drugs, alcohol, and neglect. He had six other siblings who were in the care of his biological mother while he and his twin brother were with the Krafts. One night, when his mother was in the hospital having surgery, their house burned to the ground. All six siblings perished, along with his mother's boyfriend. This was Kory's trauma, and we were able to speak openly about the pain of our childhoods. I spoke to him of my loss; he told me of his. It was so rare for me to be able to speak to someone about my father's death.

Kory became my best friend. Many Saturdays in the winter, I looked forward to each track meet so I could be out of the house and see Kory and my new friends. Kory and I became so close that we would write each other letters during the school weeks and during the seasons when track was not in session.

One summer, Kory came to visit me at my job at a nearby amusement park. He traveled nearly two hours, and I never told my parents because I knew they would not approve. This was typical of our friendship, which slipped under my family's radar for a long time. I did talk about Kory at home some, and finally my parents discovered that he was Black. My stepfather did not approve. Once he learned he began to intervene. He tossed some letters from Kory into the trash without my knowing. I'd talk to Kory and find out that he'd written letters to me that I'd never read or even seen.

Kory and I also talked on the telephone sometimes, but my stepfather would not allow me to take the call if he answered and Kory was on the other end.

One time I was in the kitchen when my stepfather answered a call from Kory. He told Kory that I was not at home and said, "don't bother calling back." I was so angry and so hurt. My stepfather had never met Kory, but the color of his skin was all he had to know.

I told Kory about my stepfather's racism, and he was so good about accepting my friendship despite it. Kory dealt with pockets of racism in school and in sports. This wasn't new to him. He never let it interfere with our friendship. He once said, "Hey, does he know I'm adopted and raised by a white family? Does that get me any points with your stepfather?" Unfortunately, that didn't change anything.

Perhaps in another time and another household the relationship could have been romantic. But I had to make it clear to Kory that I couldn't let it evolve that way, even if I wanted to. I had to tell him that my family would never accept him and they would never accept me if we dated, and I could not risk losing my family. He understood, and our friendship stayed steady. We had what I would call a very loving friendship. He's now married to a wonderful woman who teaches at-risk youth, and they live in New Jersey with two beautiful children. We still talk and text, knowing that if one needed anything, the other would be there. Only recently, he texted me that "we still had a beautiful friendship despite barriers and things like that, which tried to keep us apart."

My teenage years were tough. I struggled with home life; I struggled with the standard pressures of being in high school; I struggled with the forever nagging issue of not fully knowing who I was. I was this shell on the outside but unsure who I was on the inside. I knew I was Dee Quinn, daughter of murdered corrections officer Bill Quinn, but I didn't know enough about him to feel complete—just a few details, like how tall he was, the color of his hair, that he had a club foot, that he played sports in high school. I knew nothing of his personality, of the essence of who he was.

One of the doctors I saw for stomach issues asked once if my family and I had considered counseling. I'd wanted to do it, but my mother at first was unsure. I think she worried that counseling might open up a Pandora's box of emotions for me and that the effects would impact not only me but also our whole family.

She was very aware of my unhappiness and finally relented and agreed to counseling. I don't think there was specific grief counseling for youth then, so I assume we just looked in the phone book or some directory under counseling and found one in nearby Batavia. I was fifteen or sixteen at the time. For the first visit I literally cried and talked from the beginning of the session to the end. I had so much to say, and, finally, someone ready to listen.

What I particularly liked with the counseling was the fact that the therapist told me that I did not have to tell my parents anything we discussed. It was all confidential, he said. That provided me with some additional strength. His office was a sanctuary, a place where my tears and pain were accepted.

Unfortunately, I went only three times before my mother stopped the sessions. She questioned whether the therapy was working. She'd pick me up afterward, and I would sob for the entire car ride home. I remember her saying, "Every time I pick you up, you're so upset and it takes days for you to settle down." She didn't realize that the sessions were a cathartic release for me. She saw them as something adding to my sadness. I was too young to drive, so my therapy stopped.

Years later, I attended a memorial service at the Attica prison—a remembrance of those who lost their lives or were injured there in 1971—and I was introduced to a new member of the prison pastoral staff. The new pastor was the same man who'd been my counselor when I was a teenager. He now had some flecks of gray hair but looked much the same.

Once we became reacquainted, he asked me, "Dee, how are you doing now?"

I wanted to say, "About the same as last time you saw me," but I didn't. That would have been the truth. Much had changed, of course. I was a once-divorced and now-remarried mother of two by the time we met again. But there were still the stomach pains, occasional tearfulness, uncertainty.

As a teenager, I longed to separate myself from my father's death and the Attica uprising, while also wanting to know so much more about both. It was a contradiction I battled and would for the rest of my life. But the time would come when I would learn the details of the riot and come to know so much more.

Like everything else related to Attica, those answers would not come easy.

CHAPTER THREE

Life beyond Attica

After high school I attended nearby Genesee Community College for two years, then went to Buffalo State College where I focused on family and consumer studies and textile sciences. The cost of my college was paid for by the Lend-A-Hand fund called the Attica Fund for the children of state employees killed at Attica. The costs otherwise would have been a hardship for my family.

I did somewhat succeed in putting Attica out of my mind for my college years, though not entirely. In some classes I researched the history or wrote of my personal experience in papers. The focus of one English class assignment was a personal event that was life altering. I wrote of the riot and the murder of my father. I could tell the professor was not prepared for a paper so heavy. I don't think he was ready for something much more personal than "I recall when my cat died."

The professor had been in college at the time of the riot and had consumed the news. He knew some attorneys who represented inmates in civil suits against the state after the uprising, and he was also friends with college professor and activist Bruce Jackson, who had followed the riot and its aftermath closely, once telling the *New York Times* that the uprising was "the end of the 1960s."

"What went on at Attica was the end of the whole liberation movement," Jackson told the *Times*.

My professor's relationships with the lawyers and friendship with Jackson made him keenly interested in what I wrote. He wrote the kindest remarks in the columns of my paper, compassionate comments about the loss of my father.

My friend Kory was also a student at Buffalo State while I was there. We had talked before and we made up our minds to go to the same college. I commuted while he lived on campus. Our friendship continued, much easier to maintain now we were away from our families. There were several other Genesee Community College students who had transferred to Buffalo State, making the transition easy for me. I loved the freedom of a larger, more diverse college.

I loved fashion as a teenager, and that prompted my choice of a major. I'm not sure I would advise many people to travel such a route, but I somehow managed to craft a career out of my field of studies after graduation. In 1988, I went to work for Panama Jack Company, the popular beachwear and sun care distributor. The owner, Jack Katz, was quite the entrepreneur. Years before he'd been a football hero as a defensive lineman for the University of Florida Gators, and the company he formed in 1974 was a smashing success by the time I joined its ranks.

For Panama Jack, I traveled extensively, assisting with fabrication and design and selling the Panama Jack line. The distributor that I worked for was responsible for all sales in New York State. I traveled frequently to North Carolina, which was a major source of much of the nation's fabric, and also to Winter Haven, Florida, where the company was headquartered. Once Katz rented an entire villa at the Aspen Colorado Snowmass, a gem of a resort if you're a skier, and he hosted many of the top distributors. I remember my final leg there on a small prop plane, flying far too close to the treetops as I watched moose roam below. This was a different world from anything I'd known before, and I enjoyed the travel and the people. No one at Panama Jack knew who I was or likely cared. I enjoyed the anonymity as well.

While working for Panama Jack, I met my first husband. I married in 1990 and it would be an understatement to say I chose poorly, but I did. There was one moment on my wedding day when I realized that my stepfather, even with our discomfort with each other, perhaps understood my feelings more than I imagined. He was about to walk me down the aisle, but, moments before he did, he leaned over to me and said, "Do you really want to do this?"

I was thinking of the full church awaiting us and told him we had to go forward with the wedding. He said, "There's a car parked right outside and we can go." I think he had a sense of my unease, which still blows my mind given our differences and difficulties.

The truth was that there was a part of me that was unsure if I was doing the right thing, and my stepfather's offer was tempting. He seemed to share my questions about whether this marriage could work. It didn't, by no fault of my own.

Still, were it not for the marriage, as troubled as it was, I would not have my wonderful daughter, Aubrey, who was born in December 1993. In 1995, the divorce was final and I became a single mother.

My sister, Amy, was then dating a man who was her high school sweetheart and who came from a family of eight siblings, a man she'd ultimately marry in August 1997. Three months after my marriage fell apart, she invited me to dinner with them and her boyfriend's brother, David Miller. She insisted it wasn't a double date but just a chance to get out. I can honestly say that I was not looking forward to the night. My plan was to spend the hours with Aubrey before her bedtime, playing and reading books. After lots of encouragement from my sister, I relented and my mother watched Aubrey.

I was *not* good company. I said very little and hardly looked at David through the whole meal. I enjoyed my new life as a single mother, and I had no interest in meeting anyone. I appreciated my spaghetti dinner and talking with my sister, but I barely said two words to David.

A few months later David was back in town and came by my house and talked, acknowledging how strange and uncomfortable the dinner had been. David had also been going through a divorce at the same time. We both decided we could use a friend, and we began to talk regularly. Soon we were dating in earnest.

David worked for American Airlines. He'd started there loading luggage in the underbelly of airplanes, but soon management recognized his prowess with computers, and he helped the airline with its baggage sorting system and other computer-related needs. He was attending DeVry Institute of Technology at the time, majoring in computer information systems.

David was living in Dallas, where the company was headquartered. In those days, Aubrey and I could fly for nearly free to see him, using American Airline passes given to employees, and we'd often go to Texas to visit. Between 1995 and 1996 we dated long distance. I tried an extended stay in Texas for several weeks, uprooting Aubrey to do so, but decided I wanted her to have family—especially cousins—nearby. We returned to western New York.

David decided to come back to New York also. He later told me that he fell in love with Aubrey first, then me. I knew then he was a keeper. We married in May 1997, and in 1998 our daughter Cassidy was born.

David knew all along of my history, having learned about the death of my father even before my sister dated his brother. David has an interest in history, and, as we dated, he would ask me questions about the Attica uprising and about my life. Some of our talks were very personal, about my struggles, and some were from a more historical perspective. I had continued to read about the riot in college and was able to tell him the history that I knew from research and my own experience. But my history was often inconsistent and on unsure footing, simply because I carried so many different versions of Attica through my life.

In the years after my divorce and during my remarriage, Attica was still in the news, even though the riot had happened a quarter century before. I had left my job at Panama Jack and was working as a manager for Nutrisystem. Some days I would travel to Buffalo for the job, but more often I'd visit the main office in Rochester. On my drives, I'd hear the occasional newscasts reporting an ongoing Attica-related civil trial in a federal courtroom in Buffalo. The radio segments provided broad outlines of what the trial was about—inmates who'd been imprisoned at the time of the uprising alleging that they were brutalized after the retaking—but not a lot more. I'd also see news about the trial on the evening broadcasts from Buffalo television stations.

One of those who alleged that he'd been badly beaten after the retaking was the inmate Frank Smith, whose nickname in prison was "Big Black." The name made sense; Frank Smith was big and Black, built like a linebacker. But, during the federal trial in Buffalo, Frank Smith was just a name I'd occasionally hear in newscasts or discussions about the Attica riot. I knew little of Frank Smith other than what I'd read in some of the histories.

The allegations of torture made by Smith during the civil trial were awful. Smith claimed that he'd been individually targeted after State Police wrested control of the prison from inmates in the September 13, 1971 bloodbath—a fusillade of gunfire through a fog of tear gas. Because of his immense physique and the respect other prisoners had for him, Smith had been part of the inmate "security" team during the standoff. He and other inmates, along with a contingent of Muslim prisoners, provided protection for the hostages.

Smith had been a constant presence at the negotiations between inmates and state officials in the days after the initial uprising and before the retaking. An Associated Press photograph from September 1971 shows state Corrections Commissioner Russell Oswald seated at a table across from a line of seated and standing inmates conveying their demands for improved prison conditions. In the rear center of the photo is Frank Smith, a cloth cap on his head, wearing dark sunglasses, his hands on his hips. Clad in a white T-shirt, Smith looks both stoic and intimidating. Of the nearly two dozen prisoners in the photo, none appear as self-assured as Frank Smith. His omnipresence during negotiations convinced police that he'd been a riot organizer, and a false rumor circulated that he'd castrated a hostage.

The *New York Times*, reporting the allegations brought forth by Smith at trial, wrote that "the plaintiff...was forced to walk over broken glass, beaten with batons, locked in his cell for four days, burned with cigarettes, made to lie on a picnic table for hours with a football under his chin and threatened with castration and death."

Smith was not the only inmate alleging unimaginable brutality. As I would later discover, inmate after inmate testified that they were made to walk, barefoot and naked, the same gantlet as Smith. They, too, stepped on shattered glass and were beaten with batons by police and corrections officers.

The inmates had originally sued state officials in 1975, but it took almost twenty years of legal twists and turns to get the case to federal court. Spearheading the lawsuit was Elizabeth "Liz" Fink, a firebrand New York City civil rights lawyer who refused to let the lawsuit die. Fink had a credo that she lived by: "Dare to struggle; dare to win."

Federal Judge John Elfvin oversaw the Buffalo trial and managed to become news in the case—something I would think judges prefer not to happen.

The trial lasted ten weeks, and the jury began its deliberations in January 1992, the same time as Elfvin had a Caribbean vacation scheduled. To the dismay of many, Elfvin left on the three-week vacation and flew to Barbados. He said another judge could handle the verdict if one were delivered.

The Buffalo news broadcasts highlighted Elfvin's vacation, practically mocking his decision to travel while presiding over a trial receiving national media attention. It turned out to be a short-lived vacation. US District Judge Michael Telesca, who was the administrative judge for federal courts in Buffalo and Rochester, stepped in and contacted Elfvin.

"I called Judge Elfvin in Barbados," Judge Telesca told the *New York Times*, "…and strongly urged him to return and preside over jury deliberations personally until a verdict is released. He then would be free to return to his vacation once this is done, but not sooner."

My life would later intersect with Telesca's, brought together by the Attica uprising, and I would learn that he tended to get what he wanted in a courtroom. Some lawyers called him "the Closer" because he could arm-twist opposing parties into settlements when others had been unable to do so.

Elfvin heeded Telesca's request and returned to Buffalo for the jury verdict. The jury ruled that the abuses had occurred and determined that some of the state officials sued by inmates were culpable. That verdict set the stage for more hearings to decide how much compensation individual inmates would receive. Legal wrangling continued and it wasn't until 1997 before the damages were decided. By then, two inmates who'd been crucial to the lawsuit's filing in 1975 had died.

In 1997 the jury awarded Frank Smith $4 million. Another inmate, David Brosig, was awarded $75,000. Future hearings were planned to determine damages for other prisoners.

"This is a feeling I will never be able to express," Smith told the *New York Times*. "We finally got justice. The jury has sent a message that people everywhere need to be treated like humans, not animals."

I remember hearing of the $4 million awarded to Frank Smith. I was shocked. I held the inmates responsible for my father's death. I blamed the judicial system for the compensation, believing it was tilting unfairly toward the prisoners, and now, more and more of them would be handed millions in taxpayer money. If any family knew suffering, I felt, it was mine, but we were not in line for million-dollar awards.

However, the $4 million award for Smith was short-lived.

State officials appealed, and in 1999 a federal appellate court overturned the earlier verdicts. The appellate judges did not challenge the inmate allegations of rampant brutality. In fact, the judges wrote that there was "substantial evidence that, following the retaking" inmates had been "the victims of brutal acts of retaliation by prison authorities." But, the judges ruled, the jurors at the initial liability trial years before had been given inconsistent directions that could have caused confusion. The appellate court recognized how long the case had dragged on and urged the federal judiciary to move quickly to a new trial or resolution. The courts should sanction state officials if they tried to stretch the process out further, the judges said in the decision.

Instead, the appellate ruling prompted negotiations between the state and the inmates' lawyers. There had been attempts at settlements throughout the years, but they had gone nowhere. Now, with each passing month, more of the inmates who'd been at Attica in September 1971 were passing away. Frank Smith encouraged a settlement, even if it meant he might not see the same millions he'd been awarded in 1997.

Behind the scenes, Liz Fink had been talking to federal Judge Telesca, wondering if he could maneuver the state toward a settlement. Telesca did intervene, tasking a federal magistrate judge with trying to craft a resolution. Ultimately, Telesca himself became part of the negotiations with the Office of New York Governor George Pataki. As Telesca later recalled to historian Heather Ann Thompson, he believed the governor's office tried at first to stonewall him, unwilling to make a settlement offer of any substance. But he kept pushing, finally succeeding.

Life beyond Attica

In late 1999, the state announced a $12 million settlement for the inmates, with $4 million to be set aside for Fink and other lawyers who'd worked for the prisoners for nearly thirty years. Governor Pataki decided that Telesca would be the one to determine how much money from the $8 million should be awarded to individual Attica inmates and the families of the prisoners who'd died at Attica.

This, too, became major news. The inmates, the very people who'd started the riot and killed my father, were getting $8 million.

I was angry. I was not alone.

CHAPTER FOUR

The Radio Show

I t started with a radio show and a telephone call. I had nothing to do with either one of them.

In fact, I wasn't even listening to the radio show that would set the stage for my life for years to come. Were it not for the show, my future might have been very different.

On Saturday, January 8, 2000, only days after the announcement of the inmate settlement, radio talk show host John Carberry was doing a morning show on the station, WBTA. Carberry had a bit of a hippie vibe about him, but he also believed that government could do good. He'd been a construction worker, a reporter, a legislative aide in the state capital of Albany, even a political campaign manager.

Now he had a Saturday morning talk show on WBTA in Batavia. Each Saturday he'd talk about current local and state issues.

As I later learned, Carberry mentioned the inmate settlement of $12 million but didn't dwell on it. As he talked, his producer, Debbie Horton, took a call from a man wanting to discuss the settlement. The caller did not want to identify himself or go on the air.

On his next break, Carberry picked up the phone.

The Radio Show

The man continued to refuse to reveal his name and told Carberry that the media didn't have the whole story of the Attica riot, nor did it seem to want to know the story. The media in the past had instead perpetuated misinformation about the riot, he said.

Attica residents who were corrections officers and civilian employee survivors and their families could tell much more of the story, but no one ever asked them, he said.

"You never come here and talk to us," he said.

It was almost like a dare—come to Attica and learn more. The man hung up and Carberry went back to the radio show, never to discover who the caller was.

Carberry could not stop thinking about that call. Weeks before, he had done a remote radio talk show. He decided he'd try the same thing in Attica and make the inmate settlement the topic of conversation.

Carberry and Horton set a date for mid-February. He reached out to a woman who'd once been a guest on his show and owned a popular dining spot, the Signature Café, on Attica's Main Street.

In the days before the show, Carberry and Horton took out ads in the Batavia newspaper, the *Daily News,* informing the townspeople about the upcoming radio show. They distributed fliers around Attica, making sure WBTA promoted the remote show, while wondering if anyone would actually show up. The caller had piqued their interest, but he was only one caller. Who knew if anyone else cared?

On the Saturday morning of the show, Carberry arrived an hour early and found a back room at the café to prepare. He didn't know what to expect and whether anyone would attend. During the hour, he prepped on the history of the riot and the settlement. He had ninety minutes of airtime to fill up.

It turned out that would not be enough.

Minutes before the 9 a.m. start, Debbie Horton found Carberry and told him, "Don't be nervous." There were people, she said—a lot of them.

The café was packed. Every table was filled, and the overflow crowd was standing room only.

My family and I had learned of the radio show, and my mother, sisters, and a family friend and I decided to go, even though we were very hesitant. The radio station had a sign-in sheet for anyone who wanted to talk about their experience or the riot in general.

I remember looking around the room wondering who were these people and had their fathers been killed too? I showed up purely out of curiosity, but I was scared at the same time. What would I hear? Who would speak? Do they know me? Even though I was thirty-five years old, I was so sensitive, and I could still get upset at the mention of my father's name.

Internally, I continued to struggle with a desire to know more about my father's death, and at the same time I harbored a fear of knowing more.

Carberry served as a moderator, giving a brief introduction about why he decided to host the live show. To some people, Carberry said, the Attica uprising was "about race or social injustice or failed state policies or rebellious criminals."

"For the people to whom Attica is a home...the Attica prison uprising is a very different thing," he said. "It's a personal tragedy about violence, about loss, about trying to survive."

Many of those at the restaurant felt that the community of Attica had been unfairly portrayed as racist and bigoted in the decades after the riot. Across the nation, and much of New York for that matter, Attica was only known as the home of the prison where the nation's deadliest prison riot erupted. And, in popular culture, the riot was often painted as a racist white prison establishment pitted against Black and Latino inmates.

As I would learn at the Signature Café and later, students at Attica's high school sometimes felt so targeted when they traveled outside of the area—such as at malls in the nearby cities of Buffalo and Rochester—that they would not wear varsity letter jackets or identifying clothes. The stigma was too great and lasting, they felt, and inevitably someone would comment to them about Attica. Some Attica residents removed car dealership stickers that identified where they lived.

Among the crowd that morning were families of corrections officers killed in the riot, families such as the Monteleones and the Cunninghams. I didn't really know them personally. They were names from the books I'd read in high school and college.

My mother and I did speak briefly, answering questions from Carberry. Remembering the years of our childhood, my mother told Carberry, "My prime thing was to take care of my daughters and that was my only motive at that time. . . . This is what I figured my husband would want me to do, to see that they came first, and that's what we did."

I let Carberry know just how I felt about the settlement for prisoners. "The fact that the inmates are getting any money whatsoever is appalling," I said.

Carberry mentioned the books and the occasional films about the riot and their references to the death of my father.

"Do you ever want to escape being from Attica, being Billy Quinn's daughter?" he asked.

"Absolutely," I answered.

At Signature Café I also began to learn more about the treatment of my family and others who'd lost loved ones at Attica. I was stunned. I knew we and others had struggled, both financially and emotionally, but I now was hearing more about how little state officials had done to take care of us. One hostage who had survived, G. B. Smith, spoke of the aftermath.

"They never offered any counseling, any of that stuff," Smith said. "Now if an officer is taken hostage, they give him counseling."

Smith told how Corrections Commissioner Russell Oswald met with the hostages and other Attica employees in an Attica church one evening weeks after the riot. Oswald wanted the meeting to be unannounced publicly, with no news coverage, and the prison employees followed his order.

"The commissioner came, had a secret meeting. 'Don't tell anybody. We're going to meet at the church at 8 o'clock,'" Smith recalled.

Smith remembered Oswald's message at that meeting: "Don't worry about a thing, boys. It's all taken care of. Take six months off with pay; you don't have to worry about a thing."

What Oswald did not explain, as Smith said, was that the payments while they were off the job would be for workers' compensation, legally precluding them from litigation against the state. Smith said he was sure the state purposely duped the prison employees and their families.

"Little did we know," he said, "that killed us in any chance of suing the state. You can't sue the state if you've taken their money through workers' comp.

"I got a letter from [Governor Nelson] Rockefeller saying what a fine job I did during the riot. It's home some place in an envelope. I never bothered to put it in a frame and put it on the wall."

That was also the morning Michael and Sharon Smith walked into the café, and many in the crowd started whispering among themselves.

As I overheard the quiet chatter around me, it was clear that some people did not care for Michael Smith. I had no idea why; I had no idea who he was. I didn't know that he'd been a hostage, shot five times in the retaking.

I remembered nothing about the name of Michael Smith in my research, but in the years to come we would become fast friends, our lives intertwined.

Michael, it turned out, had long claimed that the conditions at the prison had helped spark the riot. He'd even testified about those conditions when the inmate lawsuit was in federal court in Buffalo. He was seen as an ally of the inmates by many. It was as if he'd broken from some undefined rank.

In the café, Michael and Sharon sat at a table with G. B. Smith, who'd retired, and his wife, Joan. I'd later see just how brave Michael was to come that night, to step into a room where he seemed disliked and to add his voice and his story.

When it was Michael's turn to speak, he sat down at the front table, and the room seemed to change. It wasn't as if people wanted to embrace him or befriend him, but they clearly wanted to hear him. He had a story, and, while he was telling it, you could hear a pin drop. They may have disliked him, but they still wanted to hear what he had to say.

Months before the riot some inmates had shown Michael a list of grievances they planned to give to the prison superintendent. There were demands that ranged from more than one shower a week to a request for higher wages. They also included better sanitary eating conditions—the silverware and plates were sometimes grimy and unwashed—as well as reliable medical treatment and the end to the "the escalating practice of physical brutality being perpetrated upon the inmates of New York State prisons."

The inmates were asking for basic human rights, and they trusted Michael enough to show him the "inmate manifesto," as it was later called, in which they detailed their demands.

Later that spring of 1971, the inmates presented the manifesto to the prison superintendent and the corrections department commissioner, but no one paid much attention. The demands went largely ignored. Perhaps history could have changed had someone simply listened. Perhaps my father would not have died.

As I would learn, Michael's interaction with inmates, and their grievances about conditions, were not the only signs of festering tension within the Attica walls. Other corrections officers sensed that trouble was imminent. At a roll-call meeting, employees were told to leave their personal belongings at home, items like their wallets and wedding rings. Only two days before the riot, according to the accounts of some corrections officers, leaders of the union that represented officers urged Attica Prison Superintendent Vincent Mancusi to consider a lockdown of the prison, limiting the time inmates were out of their cells because of brewing hostility from some prisoners. Mancusi refused, saying the prison was safe and would be managed as normal.

On the day of the riot, Michael was a corrections officer working in the prison's metal shop. He was swept up along with thirty-seven other prison workers and taken as a hostage to the area known as the D Yard.

There Michael was interviewed by a television news crew which, along with other media, had been allowed into D Yard, where the hostages were held. Michael had a message for Governor Nelson Rockefeller, who had refused to come to Attica and address the inmates.

Rockefeller should "get his ass here now," Michael told the interviewer.

On September 13, Michael was one of the hostages taken to the prison catwalk by would-be "executioners." The inmates wanted to send a message to Rockefeller, the corrections officials, and State Police that the prisoner demands should be met. But they also wanted amnesty for the murder of my father; and that wasn't going to happen. Rockefeller, meanwhile, continued to refuse to travel to Attica and speak with the inmates.

On that September 13 morning, as Michael recounted during the Café radio show, there were eerie quiet moments before he heard the whir of the helicopter blades overhead. He began to inhale the noxious fumes of the gas only seconds before gunfire broke out. He heard the whistle of two bullets zip by his head as sharpshooters took out the inmate executioners. He was shot four times in the abdomen by an automatic weapon and hit by a bullet in his elbow from another firearm.

Michael was then only twenty-two years old; he'd been a corrections officer for just over a year.

"We all had similar experiences in the Yard and I think that's probably something only a hostage could relate to," Michael said at the café. He recounted his wounds and his "long period of recuperation."

"I don't think I suffered more than anyone else. I think that pain is a relative thing."

Michael was not as angry toward inmates as other speakers. "The inmates at the time felt that there were issues that they needed addressed and unfortunately they expressed them through the form of a riot. . . . I can't say whether the inmates deserve compensation. It's my belief that the hostages weren't the only ones that suffered mistreatment."

Michael told of lies from state officials that he portrayed as efforts to ensure the state of New York was not considered at all responsible for what happened at the Attica prison. Some state officials had wrongly claimed immediately after the retaking that hostages who died had their throats slit by inmates. In fact, they were fatally shot in the retaking. And Michael's abdominal wounds prompted another falsehood that circulated after the retaking.

"I wasn't out of the Yard yet and they reported to the press that I was emasculated and my testicles were in my mouth," he said. "The misinformation started at that point and just compounded."

There was something about what he was saying that seemed different than what everyone else said. It wasn't that others weren't telling their own truth; they were. But I was mesmerized by Michael. I was hearing a side of the Attica riot history that I'd never heard before. The books hadn't told me much about this. My mother surely hadn't told me about this.

Michael was different than others in the Signature Café that morning. For one, he never went back to work at the prison after his long recuperation. I did not know that there were surviving corrections officers and prison employees who didn't return to Attica after the riot. My uncle Dean was a hostage, and he was out of work six months. When he went back to work, he was assigned to a gun tower, no longer in prison population.

But Michael never returned. The state gave him a date to be back on the job, but when he couldn't because of the injuries, the state instead gave him a medical retirement. He tried to sue the state, holding it responsible for his suffering, but was unsuccessful. The lawsuit seemed to be another seed of others' anger toward him. Michael challenged the long-held narrative that some in the Attica corrections officer community and larger state law enforcement community wanted to believe, the idea that the state had acted to try to ensure lives weren't lost. The state employees and families at the café did not want to believe that the government had considered their loved ones, employees of the prison, as expendable. Michael Smith told a different story. And, as others spoke at the café, there was a realization among many that they'd been treated poorly.

Michael said he did not believe there was a plan to rescue the hostages during the retaking, and I could tell that did not sit well with some in the crowd. But it made sense.

I could understand why others might not want to accept that theory. Men had died, others were left with physical wounds, and survivors had deep psychological scars. The state was supposed to be more than their employer. It should have been their protector.

Michael, as I would discover, is very reserved when he speaks; he has these pregnant pauses and puts great thought into what he's going to say. It's not an act. It's Michael wanting to ensure that his story is told honestly, no matter how painful.

And painful it was that day.

His story awoke something inside of me. I was listening and hanging on his every word. I remember thinking, "This is the *truth*; here lies the truth."

Michael's willingness to expose his own pain seemed to awaken something in others too. Some who had not originally signed up to speak decided to do so. They had suffered also, yet rarely, if ever, talked about it to their loved ones or colleagues at the prison.

When somebody tells a heart-felt truth, it's as if your body intuitively knows it. I felt that way. I could not wait for the other speakers to finish so I could introduce myself to Michael. I was so taken aback by what he had to say.

The ninety minutes WBTA had scheduled for the show had proven too few. So many people spoke that WBTA added another forty-five minutes. And when it was over, I searched for Michael and his wife, Sharon.

"Thank you," I told him. "I believe I may have finally heard the truth."

We talked, hugged, and I cried and said I may have more questions for him in the future. He said he'd answer anything he could and told me how to reach him.

I went home that night feeling there was much more to know but still unsure how much I truly wanted to know. By going to the café, maybe I had opened my own Pandora's box, just as my mother had feared would happen with counseling when I was a teenager. Be careful what you wish for, I thought.

The radio show felt like a first meeting of something, an opportunity to reconnect, and many of us agreed to meet again to discuss the inmate lawsuit. It wasn't clear if these meetings would go anywhere beyond getting together to speak aloud about long subdued grievances.

Debbie Horton, the WBTA producer, is married to Gary Horton, who was the public defender in Genesee County, where Batavia is the county seat. In his job, Horton represented indigent people accused of crimes, some of them the very individuals who could end up imprisoned at Attica. He also had come to the remote radio show and had something no one else there did—an intimate knowledge of the law.

After the turnout at the radio show, G. B. Smith and others arranged for a meeting at the American Legion in Attica. He asked Gary Horton to come talk about the inmate settlement and how the inmates had gotten so far with their lawsuit. Carberry would be there to talk about how the group, if one was to form, could get its voice heard in the government halls in Albany.

Again, I struggled with the decision of whether to go. My oldest daughter Aubrey was only seven years old and Cassidy was just two years old. I had a new husband, and I did not want to drag him into this. I worried that I could not handle these feelings and family life.

I had so much to lose, and I worried I would fall into a state of depression. Throughout my life, every bit of new information that came to me about my father could bring on a strange mix of happiness and sadness. If my mother remarked that something I had said or done reminded her of Dad, I would feel a rush of joy at learning more about my father, regardless of how trivial or how significant, and a wave of grief that I did not have him around. It may be difficult for some people to understand what even the smallest bit of new information can do to somebody who has had little or no information, or even occasional misinformation. It can be unnerving. There is an instant recognition of how little you know.

I kept thinking about whether I should go or not. I wanted to know more, but at what expense? How do you decipher the truth? I knew this could be an endless road with nothing but land mines of pain along the way.

Still I gathered the nerve and willpower to go to the American Legion with my sister. I had this feeling that I shouldn't miss this opportunity to meet all of these people—people who had known my father as a colleague and friend.

I immediately had anxiety when we reached the Legion and I saw that the parking lot was packed. I had to park along the road.

The hall, as I'd assumed, was crowded; the bar was busy. This was very different from the standard American Legion gathering; typically, the Legion was the community center home of Friday fish fries and euchre tournaments.

There were people at the bar who were obviously upset with the inmate settlement. I heard people asking how on earth the inmates—the ones who had started the riot—could be paid. Some knew the earlier jury verdict had been reversed, and they wondered why the state would now agree to restitution. Were it not for the prisoners and the riot, there would have been no injuries, no deaths. Yet, the inmates were getting millions.

I felt the same way; I didn't understand why the inmates were receiving a settlement. I had a major question I wanted answered: Would Charles Pernasilice and John Hill get money too? After all, Charles Pernasilice was convicted of assaulting my father and John Hill convicted of my father's murder. Both men were free, and I could not stand the idea that they might get paid.

G. B. Smith was one of the officers taken hostage during the uprising. Inmates yanked his nightstick from him and beat him with it. Prisoners were stripping him of his clothes when an inmate who knew Smith intervened, telling the others, "This is my motherfuckin' hostage." The inmate, worried about Smith's safety, then helped get Smith to D Yard.

G. B. would go on to become like the mayor of the group we'd eventually form. He was this extremely kind and decent man whom everyone liked. He was retired and had the time and the connections to get hold of people. To this day, I think he was the one who had originally called Carberry at WBTA.

I felt like a stranger in the American Legion. Everybody there seemed to know everybody else. Many had stayed in Attica, continuing to work at the prison. Our family had left Attica, and we'd lost much of our connection with the town and its people. We did not have the daily interactions that these people did, whether it be at their jobs or in the neighborhoods or in the supermarkets. They worked together, they visited together, their kids went to school together and played together.

I saw some people about my age and wondered whether their fathers had been killed or injured. I think there was an assumption made by a lot of people in the room that we knew everyone, but we really didn't. G. B. was working the room, saying hello to all; he was like the master mixer.

Shortly after we arrived, G. B. brought this bear of a man over to meet my sister and me. His name was Royal Thomas Morgan—and he was a twenty-three-year-old corrections officer at the time of the riot. He stood six-foot-four, probably 260 pounds. Guys at the prison and some inmates called him "Tree Trunk."

He so clearly had a story about the riot he wanted to tell me; it was as if he'd been waiting since 1971. He wasted no time that night getting to it.

He introduced himself and told me that he was a corrections officer in the hall with my father on September 9, 1971. He'd also been attacked by inmates, beaten badly. Prisoners assaulted him with his nightstick and with a two-by-four. He'd feigned unconsciousness after the inmates had stripped him of most of his uniform. After the wave of inmates moved on, he'd pulled himself up, dazed, and sat for moments, largely naked, on a radiator. He saw a pool of blood on the floor; most was his own. He'd suffered a broken wrist and a head wound that would require twenty-eight stitches. His arms had been battered as he tried to shield himself.

He saw my father nearby, unconscious on the floor. Morgan tried to lift my father up and carry him to safety at the administration building, but Morgan's injuries were too severe, the pain too acute, for him to carry my father very far. Even with his strength, his arms were essentially worthless. Morgan remembered little of what happened after.

I may have seemed under control as I listened, but I wasn't. I had a soda in my hand, and I could barely hold on to it. I felt like I was on the verge of hyperventilating.

This story rocked my world, not only because it was a stark reminder of what my father endured but it also told me something about the minutes and hours after the assault on my father. I had never thought about how my dad got out of "Times Square," the central prison hub area where he was beaten. I just assumed other corrections officers had gotten him to an ambulance.

It was at that point that I really began wondering what other information I was missing. I'd gone through college and I'd read all the books about the history of the uprising, but I'd never thought about how my dad made it to safety. As I'd learn in the months and years ahead, even this story had been omitted from the histories. Much of the story was untold; this, as I would learn, was not uncommon when it came to the Attica riot.

After talking to Morgan, I wondered how many more people I didn't know would tell me stories about my father. I knew that I'd had enough for one night, and I did not want to run into anybody else and hear about my father and his final hours.

Still, I forced myself to stay. Thankfully, no one else approached me with stories about my father's suffering.

G. B. called the meeting to order—it was the beginning of his days in organizational leadership— and G. B. and Carberry and Gary Horton took seats at the table, ready to answer whatever questions they could. G. B. gave a brief introduction: "The reason why we're here tonight as we all know is that the inmates are on track for their distribution of their $12 million and I know a lot of people aren't happy about that and we have Mr. Carberry here and we have Mr. Horton here to help us."

G. B. then asked some questions that I knew many of the others had been thinking, including: Was there any way we could stop the settlement?

Horton and Carberry were a good pair. Horton could navigate the legal issues, and because Carberry had extensive experience with the state government, where he'd worked as a chief of staff to a state assemblyman from western New York, he could respond to legislative questions. But, regardless of the passion and anger in the room, it was evident that getting the state to back off of the settlement was a long shot at best. The inmate lawsuit had been around for more than two decades, had gone to court several times, and had even ended once with a verdict for the prisoners that was later reversed on appeal. The state wanted this to go away, and $12 million probably seemed like a cheap resolution compared to the continuing legal costs.

Carberry suggested that the group rent a bus and make a trek to Albany and show up at the doors of lawmakers who wielded legislative strength. This idea didn't get very far at first. These were people who preferred to watch their government from afar, and complain about it from afar, and a trip to Albany and possible confrontations with legislators did not strike them as something they were ready to do. But, as the evening went on, more people began to warm to the idea.

I sat quietly and listened, all the time wondering if Pernasilice and Hill would get any of the $12 million. I didn't ask, though; I was still uncomfortable, still rattled from my talk with Royal Morgan.

The meeting ended after about an hour, with no clear-cut path forward but an agreement to meet again and see what ideas could be formulated. I had no idea then that I was at the birth of an organization that would soon consume much of my life, a group that would become committed to ensuring that the truths of the Attica riot—from all sides—would not be buried.

These people at the American Legion also considered themselves victims of the riot, and they were. They had been forgotten by the state because they'd done just what the state had told them to do: Go back to your families, pull yourself together, and be ready to return to work when we say it's time for you to do so. Their bosses had also encouraged them not to talk to outsiders about the riot and even to limit the talk among themselves.

While the inmates and their lawyers had fought against the state in court for years, these individuals had gone about their lives, dealing with their own pain, their own losses, their own harrowing memories.

The Radio Show

I left that night unsure whether I would return. It might mean somebody else would drop a bomb on me like the story from Royal Morgan. Being there made me keenly aware that I did not know my own history, and I didn't like the way that it made me feel. I wondered if all those people knew who they were, because I really had no idea who I was, other than simply the daughter of slain Corrections Officer William Quinn.

I also continued to think about Michael Smith and what he had said at the Signature Café. Somewhere there was a truth about the Attica riot, facts about the death of my father that I did not know and that had been kept from me.

And I wanted to know for certain the answer to my question: Would Charles Pernasilice and John Hill get paid? If so, could I stop it from happening?

CHAPTER FIVE

My Father's Killers

While the Attica riot was a mostly unspoken topic among my mother, my sisters, and myself, there was one aspect we discussed and found agreement: It didn't seem right that John Hill and Charles Pernasilice would receive money—any money—from the inmate settlement. There was $8 million to be divided; who knew how much money they could pocket?

The two had originally been accused of fatally beating my father with a wooden object, likely a board, and had been identified by inmates and officers alike. Some of those identifications were tenuous and unreliable, it would turn out, while others held up in court.

For us, Hill was of greater concern than Pernasilice. John Hill was the man a jury had convicted of the murder of my father. How could he be rewarded? It seemed a reopening of a deep family wound, yet another injustice we would have to endure.

When I was a teenager and first read and learned about the beating of my father, little was said in the household about John Hill. All I remember hearing was that he was Puerto Rican and Indian (this was before the days of Native American as a more common identifier). I don't know why this mattered, except that, in my home, one's ethnicity and race could be considered significant, though usually for the wrong reasons. (As it turned out, Hill was not Puerto Rican. His mother was Mohawk/Cree and his father Italian American.)

What also had long hurt our family was the fact that John Hill served very little prison time for the murder of my dad. In December 1976, only a year after Hill's conviction, New York State Governor Hugh Carey decided to close the books on the Attica riot by halting prosecutions and granting amnesty, pardons, and commutations for anyone already convicted or accused of Attica-related crimes. Some in the State Police were then being targeted for possible prosecutions for crimes during the retaking—including allegations of cold-blooded murder of prisoners who were lying prone on the ground when shot—and Carey's actions ensured there would be no prosecutions of law enforcement. He also allowed John Hill to eventually go free, commuting his sentence for the killing of a peace officer.

After the meeting at the American Legion in March 2000, I reached out to attorney Gary Horton to help me understand just what the settlement meant, how it would be disbursed, and whether we could somehow put a brick wall in front of any payment to Hill and Pernasilice.

I called Gary at his office as the Genesee County Public Defender, and he explained to me the nuances of the settlement, expanding on what he'd said at the American Legion. The settlement was much like the resolution of a personal injury lawsuit, he explained. The inmates who were in the Yard when the State Police rushed into the prison on September 13, 1971, were the victims. Many suffered lifelong injuries; some, as testimony showed in the trial in Buffalo, were ruthlessly beaten and abused. Then there were the families of the inmates who were fatally shot. They, too, would be compensated.

Parsing Hill and Pernasilice out from the settlement would be unlikely, Gary told me. They were in the Yard, so they were part of the injured party.

They had as much right to payments as did any of the other nearly 1,300 prisoners who had made claims against the state during the civil litigation.

After talking with Gary, I knew the odds were long that we could block payments. But I was determined to find a way. Not many people in my family thought I could turn this around. My grandfather Willard said, "DeeDee, you can't fight City Hall." I told him, "Grandpa, you can fight City Hall. It's just a matter of whether you win or not."

With the settlement approved, it was clear that the one person who would play a significant role in the inmate payments was Rochester-based federal Judge Michael Telesca. At that point in early 2000, Telesca was preparing to hold a series of hearings over the summer months during which those seeking restitution could testify. They did not have to testify—they could also make a claim for restitution with a legal documentary filing—but Telesca wanted to give the inmates a chance to tell their stories in a courtroom forum.

As I would learn, this was typical of Telesca. He was a law-and-order appointee of President Reagan, and he held the Constitution dear. He believed that the inmates deserved a day in court, regardless of whatever crimes had landed them at Attica. He once said, "The Eighth Amendment does not stop at the prison gates," meaning that inmates were ensured the same protections against "cruel and unusual punishment" as anyone else. But my knowledge of Telesca's history would come later; right now, he was the man I thought could bring a halt to money for John Hill and Charles Pernasilice.

I decided to write Judge Telesca and let him know how my family and I felt. In early February, I drafted the letter to him on behalf of me and my mother, with her permission.

"This letter is to introduce you to four of the 'real' victims of the Attica Riot," I wrote. "We are what remains of the Quinn family. Billy Quinn left behind a pregnant wife, Nancy, and three daughters, Deanne, Christine and Amy (unborn). "

I told him how Hill and Pernasilice had "received a second chance" because of Governor Carey. "Billy Quinn did not," I stated.

My anger coursed throughout the letter: "We ask you, as you settle this atrocity with a financial pay off, to consider our lives over the past 29 years. Our father was denied taking part in our childhoods, our graduations, our birthdays, and our marriages. Think about a daughter that will never know her father. The inmates took away part of our lives that we can never recover.

"Your job is to serve and protect the public, not pay off convicted murderers. We are pleading with you to reconsider the settlement. We believe that the inmates deserve no money at all. Please make the right decision."

I signed the letter from the wife and daughters of William E. Quinn, unsure just what—if anything—to expect next.

To my surprise, I received a call from Judge Telesca's office within days. The call came from a woman I would come to know well—Judge Telesca's longtime secretary, Joan Countryman. I nervously answered, feeling as if I were receiving a call from the president. Who gets calls from federal judges, after all?

Judge Telesca was gracious as he heard me out, listening as I told him why my family was hurt by the possibility of payments to Hill and Pernasilice. He made me no promises in reply—for all I knew he planned on doing nothing afterward—but he appeared understanding and sympathetic.

Though uncertain whether my pleas would make any difference, I knew the letter had touched enough of a chord with Judge Telesca to compel him to call me. That was a start.

The fact that John Hill could be rewarded was only one slight to our family. Had he faded into the woodwork, living a quiet life in which we rarely had to hear his name, then perhaps he could have been somewhat forgotten. Instead, John Hill had emerged in his post-incarceration days as a civil rights activist for Native Americans and other causes. He had taken the name Dacajeweiah, or "Splitting the Sky," and moved to Canada. He touted his time at Attica as if a badge of honor.

In 1995, Hill was a prominent protester at what was called the Gustafsen Lake Standoff in British Columbia, Canada—a monthlong impasse between the country's indigenous people and the Royal Canadian Mounted Police. Sparking the standoff was a disagreement between a rancher and a tribe wanting to use private land for a ceremonial purpose. Hill later would also be arrested in Canada for trying to make a "citizen's arrest" of President George W. Bush in 2009 at the Telus Convention Centre in Calgary. Hill claimed Bush had committed "crimes against humanity."

Even before his transformation into an activist, Hill had become something of a liberal cause celebre during his trial for the murder of my father. Defending Hill was the prominent leftist lawyer William Kunstler, who long had been willing to take on political cases, as exemplified by his defense in the case of the Chicago Seven the year before the Attica riot.

Hill and Pernasilice had been tried together in 1975, with Pernasilice having his own high-powered defense—former US Attorney General Ramsey Clark. The defense lawyers successfully discredited many witnesses during the trial, showing that some inmates who said they witnessed the killing of my father had expected to be rewarded with transfers or paroles.

One of the witnesses for the prosecution was Royal Thomas Morgan, the same corrections officer who later would tell me how he'd tried to help my father. At trial, Morgan identified Hill as the man significantly responsible for the death of my father. The defense attorneys worked to undermine the testimony, reminding the jury that Morgan, by his own admission, had not been clearheaded because of his serious injuries. Nor had Morgan been as specific in interviews shortly after the riot about who the assailants had been.

Years later, as I ventured back into the history of Attica—and after I had been so shaken by the story Morgan told me at the American

Legion—Morgan assured me in a conversation that he was certain Hill was the man most responsible for my father's death. He told me how, in the weeks before Hill's trial and during the trial, he received death threats over the phone. He grew so worried that he bought a gun for his wife and taught her how to use it.

Morgan had been working in the barber shop area of the prison metal shop on September 9. He was then on "vacation relief," filling in for officers who were off work. Sgt. Edward Cunningham, who would be taken hostage and fatally shot in the retaking, had heard of a fight breaking out in the area known as the prison's A Block. Morgan gave his keys to Cunningham, a precautionary move, and Morgan went to respond.

En route, he was assaulted by the surge of inmates who stripped him of his uniform. He managed to move on from there, and, at the prison's Times Square, he saw Hill and a man he later identified as Pernasilice around my father, beating him. Hill was beating my father with a two-by-four, Morgan said.

Hill then rushed him, hitting him with the same two-by-four and knocking his glasses from his head.

Later, as the State Police plainclothes division—the Bureau of Criminal Investigation—investigated my father's death, the investigators showed Morgan a photo lineup to identify those who'd attacked my father. He picked out Hill, whom he knew well from the prison. During our conversation, I asked him if he could have misidentified Hill. He never wavered. He was sure it was Hill whom he saw. He was absolutely staunch about it.

After the riot, Morgan was moved up the corrections officer transfer list, and he went to the Auburn Correctional Facility. As he told me of his exodus from Attica, he "never looked back."

The jury in 1975 clearly believed Morgan and other prosecution witnesses, convicting Hill and Pernasilice. In my adulthood, there have been people who have tried to get me to reconsider Hill's guilt. I have decided not to revisit the evidence against him or his claims of innocence. I don't want anybody to have that kind of power over me.

In 2000, however, I had no doubts of Hill's guilt, and the fact that Judge Telesca had called me at home in response to my letter seemed a positive sign. Still, he'd given me no assurances during the call that he would do anything.

But Telesca did listen to us. Weeks after we spoke, I received another call from his secretary, Joan Countryman. She told me that "the judge would like me to let you know their names will not be in the final paperwork." I assumed this meant that Hill and Pernasilice would receive nothing.

I later learned that Judge Telesca had managed a backdoor effort, having the lawyers make payments to Hill and Pernasilice from their own money. The judge knew that protests of the settlement, should I or others choose to do so, would likely be a public relations setback, and he wanted the hearings to proceed in the summer of 2000 without rancor or opposition. He walked a fine line, and he was very good at it.

I've grown to appreciate what Judge Telesca did for me and my family. I now recognize that Hill and Pernasilice had a legal right to be part of the settlement, and there was little that we could do to prevent it. I was thankful that he kept their names out of the final settlement.

This would be far from the last time when Judge Telesca would hear my story. In those early months of 2000, neither he nor I could envision what was on the horizon. As he prepared to listen to testimony from the Attica inmates, those of us who had gathered for the radio show and again at the American Legion decided to continue our meetings. Somehow, with the ugly history of the Attica riot about to be aired in a courtroom again, we had been forgotten.

We decided we would not stay forgotten for long.

CHAPTER SIX

Attica Families Reunite

With hearings on the inmate settlement only months away, scheduled for the summer in Judge Telesca's Rochester, New York, courtroom, it was clear that the likelihood of changing the $8 million payout to the inmates was, basically, nonexistent. But that realization didn't stop our meetings. Instead, there was a growing consensus that the prison employee survivors of the riot, and the families of those who died, had been ignored for years. We had been like good little sheep, told by the state to remain quiet and get on with our lives. And, for nearly thirty years, that was just what we'd done.

That was about to change.

After the gathering at the American Legion, G. B. Smith, working with Gary Horton and others, scheduled more meetings. I continued to go, finding myself growing more connected to these men and women who, only months before, I did not know at all. Our mutual experience, albeit an agonizing experience, bound us together.

The meetings moved from the American Legion to the Quality Work Life (QWL) building on Attica prison grounds, located on property between the prison and the superintendent's house. The single-story building had long been a cavernous party hall for prison employees and families, used for wedding receptions, graduation parties, baby showers, staff retirement parties, fundraisers, and other events. The Attica prison administration gave us permission to move our meetings to QWL, and, for years to come, that would be our hub.

I was meeting people who had lived comparable lives to mine, people who, as the years continued, I considered more as family than random people with a similar story. At the meetings were people, like me, who were children of slain prison employees. We had prison employee spouses too. And we had hostages. We even had names for some of the groups within our crowd. There were the "five dayers," the men who'd been held hostage throughout the duration of the standoff and survived. There were the "injured and released," men whom the inmates let go in the early hours of the uprising. The meetings were an outlet for people to meet, to reunite, simply to talk.

Often the best conversations happened early, during brief social gatherings before we moved to the more formal stage. It was often during these casual moments when I would learn more about my father.

It didn't take long for my hesitancy about the meetings to fade. It was as if a hole within me was being filled, as if I were continuing the counseling that I so badly wanted as a teenager. I met people who'd attended high school with my father, and my picture of how he'd live his life deepened and expanded. They shared, and I soaked in all they had to say.

Much like my teenage counseling sessions, I would often find myself in tears at the meetings. At one meeting, we decided that our group should have a name, and we recorded the group member suggestions on a flip pad. The Forgotten Victims of Attica became a popular choice to many. I was not one of them. Despite my hardships, I did not consider myself a victim. I suggested we look for other choices, though I had no idea what. Gary Horton turned to me and said, "If you are not a victim, then what are you?"

"I don't know," I answered, honestly.

I then started crying. I *was* a victim.

I was far from the only person who found the meetings emotionally stressful, yet necessary at the same time. Kentt Monteleone, for one, wanted to know everything he could about the riot—the trauma, the good, the bad, the ugly.

Kentt's father, John Monteleone, had also died at Attica. A civilian employee who was an industrial foreman at the prison, John Monteleone was taken hostage on September 9 from the metal shop, and, during the retaking, he was shot in the chest. The bullet ripped through his aorta and punctured his lung. The Ruger linked to Monteleone's death was a personal side arm of a fellow corrections officer, who said he was shooting at inmates. Kentt was then seven years old and his family, much like mine, had tried to bury Attica through the years by rarely if ever talking about it. At the meetings, Kentt discovered a close high school friend of his with her own riot connection that he'd never known.

"When I walked up, she looked at me, I looked at her, and she said, 'What are you doing here?'" Kentt later recalled. "I said, 'Well, my father was a hostage. What are you doing here?' 'Well, my father was a hostage.'"

"We had known each other for our whole lives, and this was never brought up."

Kentt would ask many questions of his father's former colleagues, and of their family members, then sometimes storm out of the meetings when the answers proved overwhelming. Yet he and I continued to return, regardless of the hurt the meetings could bring. Years later, Kentt would talk of the meetings and the people he got to know there, people who had the same feelings he and I had. "I wish this group would have met earlier," Kentt said. "I spent much of my life being really pissed off."

I understood how Kentt felt. I went, I cried, I returned.

The Prison Guard's Daughter

Kentt's older sister, Karol, told of the call from the prison on September 13, 1971, informing the family that John Monteleone had been killed. Whoever called passed the devastating news on to Karol. She was only fourteen. She simply answered the telephone, and they gave this teenage girl the news that her father was dead. She collapsed on the floor screaming, throwing the phone.

There was so much trauma being shared. And many of the families were left poor after the riot. Many of the families who were left without fathers and husbands had four to eight children, and they were living well below the poverty line.

Then there were the families of the hostages who survived. They had their own trauma. Wives would tell how the men that they'd married were not the same men who came home after the riot. One hostage transformed from a gentle giant into a horrendous nervous wreck. When he returned to the prison, he would write out every task for the day on small pieces of paper that he carried in his pocket. He had an overwhelming fear that he would forget something on the job, and his pockets were littered with scraps of paper that his wife would discover when she washed clothes.

One survivor, John Stockholm, had gone to my father's funeral, then left when he heard my mother ask his wife just how he was doing. "I looked at her and couldn't face her," he later remembered of seeing my mom. "How was I the lucky one to survive when he died with so many others?"

When John Stockholm would see John Monteleone's wife at the grocery store, he would again be beset with the same feelings of guilt. He would quickly go to another aisle to avoid her.

"My kids have grown up, played sports with these children [of slain hostages]," he would later say. "And to this day I still say why? Why [me]?"

The post-traumatic stress disorder that these people experienced was similar to that of combat veterans, yet we expected them to return to work in totality—mentally prepared, taking care of themselves physically, and ready to get back on the job as if nothing had happened. Some were promised better positions in the prison, as if the state were bribing them to return and pretend to be whole.

There was also guilt for the survivors and their families. The wives whose husbands came home knew that my mom's husband or Mrs. Monteleone's had not come back. It was another layer of suffering. Those who survived suffered. The families of those who did not survive suffered.

As we shared stories, we also shared the occasional laugh—direly needed humor. In the 1990s, Mark Cunningham, the son of a slain hostage, and his wife Laurie had owned The Tipperary, a popular bar across the street from the prison, where Mark also worked as a corrections officer. He told me that a man once came to the bar, claiming to be related to my dad, and then talked about the riot. He spoke of my father's murder, saying that it likely would not have happened had my dad treated inmates better.

Mark knew my father's history at the prison and his reputation as a corrections officer who treated inmates with dignity.

"I threw him out the door," Mark told me. "I can't remember if the door was open or not." Apparently Mark had replaced the front door to the bar several times during his ownership.

Michael and Sharon Smith also became regulars at the meetings, and I saw Michael's distrust of our purpose begin to melt away as the weeks passed. At the café, Michael had been willing to challenge the state and question its treatment of its employees. At that point, his stance appeared somewhat insolent to us; few were questioning how we'd been treated. Instead, our anger was directed at the inmate settlement. But the more we met and the more we talked, the more we grew to realize that state officials had turned their backs on the men who'd given their lives at Attica and on those who'd lived through it. Michael was unbudging in his resentment toward the state, and the group found itself becoming more accepting of his beliefs. Not all agreed with Michael that the prison conditions before the riot were the trigger, but they could accept his anger about the treatment of prison employees after the uprising.

The meetings would start at 7 p.m., and many nights I would not pull into my driveway until 10 p.m. or 11 p.m. There were nights when David would ask if maybe I'd had enough and whether I should stop going. He was always worried about my emotional health. But I couldn't stop. Some days after meetings I would call hostage survivors Gary Walker or John Stockholm and ask them to repeat stories they'd told, just to be sure I'd understood. Then I'd ask more questions.

My mother decided to accompany me, and, to my surprise, she continued to want to go. For most of her life she hadn't investigated or inquired about the riot because it was too painful. She was now in something of a learning phase. For her, Attica had been a closed book. I knew more because I'd spent time in high school and college reading about the riot, and now Mom was asking me for information.

Most importantly, she talked to other widows, including the wives of slain hostages John Monteleone and Carl Valone. Theirs was an experience that very few others could relate to, and now, they were finding solace in the stories and embraces of each other. After meetings, as we drove home, my mother would often revisit some of the conversations she'd had, trying to sort out what she was learning. "DeeDee, do you think this is true?" she'd ask of some of what she'd been told. There were times, unsurprisingly, when the meetings were too much. I would call her, planning to pick her up for the drive to Attica, and she'd tell me, "DeeDee, I don't think I can go tonight."

As purifying as the newfound camaraderie and friendship were, we still needed a direction. We knew that the inmates now had their day in court, and despite our anger there was nothing we could do. We needed goals and a purpose, and, as the weeks passed, and as we accepted the name of Forgotten Victims of Attica (FVOA), we began to map out a path.

John Carberry and Gary continued to provide their expertise–Carberry with advice as to how to traverse the politics of the state capital of Albany and Gary with legal insights. We'd ask Gary if we had any chance at legal recompense or had we waited too long, and he would do the research and return with answers at the next meeting.

From the outset, Gary explained how the inmate settlement was locked in. The state had obviously decided that a settlement was the better alternative than returning to court. The federal appellate judges had been very pointed when they reversed the earlier rulings in favor of the inmates. The evidence of abuse was ample, the judges said, so the state should be prepared to get back into court quickly. The other alternative was to settle, and that's just what happened.

Later, Gary would admit that he thought the state had gotten off cheaply with a "lowball" settlement of $12 million, but he kept that opinion to himself at our meetings. He also did not know much of the history of the Attica riot, so he was cautious in his answers to our questions. He provided information instead of advocacy, though he also thought we, too, had been mistreated.

Carberry and Gary helped convince us that any success we could have would be through political and not legal means. We knew that we needed to amass public support for whatever we decided to do, and to press state lawmakers. There was talk early of some restitution for the families, and that became one goal. But that was not enough to ease our suffering. We talked about restitution figures but discussed other possibilities, such as apologies and counseling for those who might want it.

Deciding upon our goals was not easy. Many in the group wanted unanimous consensus, but the discussions over our goals could become intensely heated, stretching out and fraying nerves. I would ask, "Can't we just do a majority? I can't take this anymore." But we continued to seek consensus, and somehow, we succeeded.

At the early meetings, the thought of approaching state lawmakers proved intimidating to many of us, but we continued to warm to the idea, especially with Carberry encouraging us. We began to set our goals high: Not only would we meet with state legislators but we also wanted a meeting with then-Governor George Pataki. First, we would carve out our demands. Then we would head to Albany.

We'd reached a crucial juncture; we would be voiceless and invisible no more.

CHAPTER SEVEN

Demands of
the Forgotten Victims

The Forgotten Victims of Attica meetings were a steady reminder of the abysmal treatment of Attica employees and their families in the aftermath of the riot. Hostage survivors had stories to tell, as did widows. My uncle Dean received a check from the state on October 28, 1971. It was for $27.50, which, according to the accompanying letter, "represents meal allowances for the period you were held hostage." He and the other men held hostage were not paid an entire day's pay for each of the days that they were captive; the state decided to pay them for only sixteen hours for each day, rather than the full twenty-four hours they were held. The state assumed they slept for the other eight hours, time deemed not-on-the-clock.

For decades, the families and prison employees had accepted these insulting bureaucratic decisions, content to return to work and move on with life. Few had discussed the treatment, nor seriously considered how little the state had done for them.

FVOA changed that, and, as we prepared to meet with lawmakers, we had to decide just what we wanted. At our developmental meetings, we'd write proposals on flip charts—what should we ask of state legislators, why are we seeking this—and debate the ideas, still pushing for consensus rather than simply majority support. We'd spend hours talking of the pros and cons of our prospective demands, sometimes with the meetings heated. Yet somehow, we managed to mend the fractures that would occur in our membership and forge on.

The inmate settlement was what had given birth to our organization, and we put some of our focus on whether we, too, should receive restitution. On this point, there was not opposition; restitution was the one demand with quick consensus.

What was unclear was what amount of restitution would be fair. In that case, we had some guidance from a lawsuit one of the widows had filed against the state of New York. Lynda Jones had accused the state of "excessive force" in its retaking of prison grounds. Her husband, Herbert Jones, had been a civilian accounting clerk at the prison. He was taken hostage and fatally shot in the head on September 13, 1971. The couple then had a twenty-month-old daughter.

As I'd learned, after the riot the state paid widows and survivors from the state workers' compensation fund. The state did not disclose to the recipients that by accepting the initial and subsequent checks that they were legally making what is known as "an election of remedy." What this meant was that they could not sue the state, just as G. B. Smith had said at Signature Café. Accepting the payments prohibited them from doing so.

Lynda Jones, however, did not cash the initial checks she received.

Jones had told a friend of one paltry check she had received from the state which, exactly like the one for my uncle, was presented as costs for the meals for her slain husband while he was a hostage. The friend told her employer, a local lawyer named William Cunningham, about the check, and he found it odd as well as heartless.

Cunningham encouraged Jones not to cash the check while he researched the retaking. He decided that the state should not be able to dodge responsibility for the deaths at Attica. Within a year of the riot, he had sued the state on Jones's behalf. The lawsuit bounced through appeals and ended nearly 10 years later with a $550,000 judgment for Lynda Jones. With interest and other costs, the payment to Lynda Jones totaled slightly more than $1 million.

Some members of our group did not know about the Lynda Jones lawsuit and victory in court. We decided to use her $1 million award as the basis of our demand for restitution. We had fifty families that made up the FVOA, and each had suffered their own hardships. We set $50 million as our demand.

The more we talked about how the widows and surviving state workers had accepted workers' compensation without knowing the legal ramifications, the angrier we became.

Ann D'Arcangelo Driscoll, whose husband John D'Arcangelo was a slain hostage, remembered Corrections Commissioner Russell Oswald coming to her home shortly after her husband's death and telling her how urgent it was that she signed the papers to provide some financial security for the future. Unlike many others, she was actually told that it would be workers' compensation, but she was not told about the long-term ramifications—the inability to pursue legal action against the state—of taking the money.

To add insult to injury, investigators from the state once went to her seven-year-old daughter's school and asked the youngster about her identity, apparently as some kind of investigation to ensure the family was not committing fraud against the state. They took the girl from the class, causing a minor disruption. The teacher explained to the other children that her father had been killed at Attica.

When the young girl returned to class, some classmates told her that her father must have been a bad person because only "bad people" were at Attica. The girl was so distraught that she asked her mother if they could change their name.

Families had been financially stretched thin, with the workers' compensation payments barely covering expenses. Many relied largely upon Social Security payments for basic needs. The widow of one slain hostage was left with unfinished home renovations that had been started by her husband. In the years after her husband's death, her children would pick up returnable aluminum cans along the road for the cash they could get.

Lynda Jones, we knew, had been the sole widow able to sue the state. We had no idea whether $50 million was a realistic demand or not for our restitution, but we knew we needed some benchmark to explain asking for any amount. If anyone asked us where we got that figure from, we could answer that we used the Lynda Jones verdict for our decision.

We also considered asking for state-funded counseling for FVOA members. While agreeing to restitution was easy, the discussions over counseling were more complicated.

There were members who were insistent that they had no need for counseling and would not use it were the state to offer it. Their attitude was that they'd made it this far without therapy, so they had no use for it now.

Others, like me, saw the value. I've always known the value of counseling, and I'm definitely going to accept it if free. I have never forgotten my few short therapy sessions when I was a teenager, and I know how valuable they were. Rarely could I unburden myself of my emotions; in the therapist's office, I could.

For me, the counseling demand was exceptionally important, and I pushed as hard as anyone that it be on the list of demands. Those who believed they had no need for it eventually saw how much it meant to others, and they eventually came around. They could choose to use it or not if the state consented.

So, counseling joined the list of demands.

We also requested that the state open all Attica-related records, though there was no certainty as to what was still sealed and what wasn't.

Grand jury proceedings that had been halted when Governor Carey ended Attica-connected prosecutions were still sealed, as were some of the investigative reports that scrutinized the state's actions during the retaking.

Nobody in our group really knew what was available, but some of the members were desperate to see if there were records that mentioned their husband, father, brother, uncle. There was little opposition internally to this demand.

Another demand, one that spurred hours of back-and-forth, was a formal apology by the state for its actions at Attica. I was strongly in support. For me—and other members, like Michael Smith—an apology would mark a fresh beginning. It wouldn't reverse the tragic decisions made by state officials, but it would be an acknowledgement that someone in a position of power—even decades later—recognized our pain and could say, "We're sorry, and we take some responsibility."

Gary Horton continued to be active with FVOA, and he'd invited an Albany-based lawyer, Jonathan Gradess, into the fold. Since 1978, Jonathan had been executive director of the nonprofit New York State Defenders Association, which was established to ensure reliable legal representation for the indigent. As the public defender for Genesee County, Gary had worked closely with Jonathan.

Jonathan Gradess and Gary were both left leaning politically, while many in our membership were staunch conservatives. Yet there was a unifying belief that we had been wronged, and any political chasm that might exist was irrelevant. Jonathan, in fact, would become one of the most vocal supporters of an apology, and he also had Albany connections because of his work there. Through the years, he often lobbied, hounded, shamed, and swore at lawmakers in Albany on our behalf.

Apologies had historical precedence, Jonathan would say. Former West German Chancellor Willy Brandt apologized for the Holocaust and President Gerald Ford for the American internment of Japanese.

"If President Bill Clinton can apologize for inaction in Rwanda, and the Khmer Rouge can apologize for the slaughter of two million Cambodians, surely New York can apologize for Attica," Jonathan would later write.

In 2019, almost two decades after I first met Jonathan, he died of pancreatic cancer. He was called "the patron saint of public defenders" in an obituary in the *New York Times*. As I write this, we still have no apology from the state and continue even now to push for one. I initially thought an apology would be one of the most likely demands that the state would agree to. Instead, it's been one of the hardest. Now, I want the apology as much for Jonathan as I do for FVOA.

Our list of demands ended with a request for an assurance from the state that we could hold a memorial service on prison grounds each September 13. We also wanted that assurance written into corrections law, so that a change of administration at the prison or the state corrections department couldn't reverse the policy. Having the state corrections law amended so that families of the Forgotten Victims could congregate on that day, we decided, would be huge for us.

In the years immediately after the riot, corrections officers had raised money for a monument on prison grounds—located near the entrance—that remembered and memorialized the men who lost their lives at Attica. The marble monument stands more than six feet tall, and beneath it are buried all of the prison keys found in the Yard after the riot. They rekeyed the entire prison and gathered up the old keys and buried them.

The words on the memorial, from poet Robert Burns, read: "Man's inhumanity to man makes countless thousands mourn."

The corrections department and state of New York did not purchase the memorial. Instead, it was funded by corrections officers, prison employees, and community members, with stone provided by Marley Funeral Home in Attica, the same funeral home that handled the burial and services for my father, as well as those of a number of slain hostages.

Demands of the Forgotten Victims

There had been a memorial service on the grounds for years, an event organized and overseen by corrections officials. An honor guard was posted for the service and the fallen remembered.

One of our members, corrections officer Mark Cunningham, remembered that prison administrators decided years after the riot that they no longer wanted to continue the formal remembrance. It again was another blow to the victims. Mark was especially angered; his father, Edward Cunningham, was a corrections officer and sergeant at Attica who was taken hostage and killed in the retaking.

But, even if nothing formal was scheduled at the prison, every September 13, at the end of the 5 p.m. inmate count, officers would line up in a queue, then march by the memorial and salute. While the prison administration may have decided to try to rid itself of the legacy of Attica, the corrections officers ensured that it would not be forgotten.

We wanted a ceremony resumed, and we wanted to control it. Corrections could do its own ceremony if it so chose, but we would call for an event organized annually by FVOA. If we wanted a small ceremony, we would have a small ceremony. If we wanted something bigger, then we would have something bigger.

Mostly, we wanted an acknowledgement that we could not let the anniversary go by ignored and forgotten. Otherwise, the lives of these men could also be ignored and forgotten by the community at large. We could not allow that.

When we'd reached consensus on the demand for a yearly ceremony, we decided that we had enough to approach lawmakers. We called our demands the "Five Point Plan for Justice." We wanted the state to provide restitution, to offer counseling for those who wanted it, to open any Attica records still closed to the public, to ensure an annual FVOA memorial ceremony on prison grounds, and to apologize.

In the months after, we decided not to wait for the state to decide whether to provide counseling. It was apparent that some in our group—me included—could benefit from therapy, and we were unsure whether the state would ever agree to pay for counseling. We'd been approached by two area clinical social workers, Bonnie Collins and Trina Laughlin, who'd offered to assist us with counseling sessions. They arranged group sessions, which shrunk in size as some FVOA members were not ready to open up about their trauma. I would continue to meet individually for years with Trina. As the task force gathered momentum, my sessions with her helped keep me sane, as I dealt with what became my more significant role with FVOA at the same time as I was learning more of my father's life and death.

A local state legislator, Republican Assemblyman Dan Burling, was aware of our group and communicated some with Gary Horton and our members. He knew that restitution was one of our demands, and he took it upon himself to see if he could get his legislative colleagues onboard.

He collaborated with a Republican state senator, Dale Volker, who represented the region where the Attica prison was located. Burling seemed genuinely sincere about doing what he could for us. Volker also took up our cause, but while he appeared publicly sympathetic, he often seemed unwilling to give his full power to our efforts. In one phone call Volker told me, "Dee, we just can't give you money." He would not get behind any restitution demand close to $50 million.

In the spring of 2000, he and Burling helped secure $50,000 in the governor's proposed budget for each of the widows, though they had sought at least $1 million. Also tucked into the proposed bill awarding the $550,000 to 11 widows were assurances that they could receive no additional future restitution.

It was up to the widows whether to accept the offer. For many of the widows, $50,000 was a lot of money, and we recognized just what the money could mean for them. But they realized and acknowledged that the offer did not help all of the families. What about the surviving hostages and their families? They had suffered also. Michael Smith, for one, had been shot five times, his stomach ripped apart by the gunfire, and he could never shake the nightmares of Attica. Others had similar post-traumatic stress. Those days in September 1971 could never be purged from their memories. Even though they often kept silent about what they'd survived, they would sometimes hear the gunfire and see the falling of bodies around them. They had survived the brutal chaos, but they had not survived unscarred.

The widows talked for hours about the state's offer. As always, we wanted consensus, but we left this decision solely to the widows.

In the end, consensus was what we got. The widows unanimously declined the offer.

CHAPTER EIGHT

Our Lobbying Begins

In the early morning hours of May 23, 2000, we packed a Greyhound bus with more than fifty Forgotten Victims of Attica members for the four-hour drive to the New York State capital of Albany. Many of the widows, hostages, and family members had chosen to come, and we wanted to be considerate of their age, but there was only so much we could do to keep the day from being draining for all. We knew the day would be taxing and exhausting. We were asking our older members to make a four-hour drive, walk around the entire capital, lobby lawmakers, and then head back along the New York State Thruway for another four-hour drive home. We also had sent out a release to media, alerting outlets that we planned a press conference about who we were, what we wanted, and why.

My mother was among the widows. With each meeting of the FVOA, she showed more willingness to tell the world that she'd been wronged. Thirty years before, she had not done so. She had a family to raise then, and she tried to put the Attica riot in the rearview mirror. But with each story of hardship told at the FVOA meetings, with other widows recalling how they'd been abandoned by the state, her fortitude grew stronger.

She would not be one of the more active or vocal members—that was not her nature—but she made it clear that she wanted FVOA to succeed, and she wanted to be part of it.

We gathered that morning—the crack of dawn—at a fire hall in Alexander, a village between Attica and the Thruway. Some FVOA members had already driven a half hour or an hour to the fire hall, and we would also make several stops along the Thruway to pick up other FVOA members.

We were building a group of powerful allies. The New York State Correctional Officers & Police Benevolent Association, the union for correctional officers, had rented the Greyhound for our trip. Rick Harcrow, the president of NYSCOPBA, as it is known, had learned about our efforts from colleagues of and was fully onboard. NYSCOPBA would be by our side for years to come; it still is.

Before the trip we had reached out to lawmakers whom we believed could help our cause. We divided up appointments among our members. We would talk to Republicans, Democrats, upstate legislators, downstate legislators. We particularly highlighted members of the corrections committees in the two houses of the New York Legislature, the Senate and Assembly.

The state Senate was then controlled by Republicans and the Assembly by Democrats, many of them from the New York City area. The downstate lawmakers knew of the inmate lawsuit—inmate attorney Liz Fink and many of the inmates, including Frank "Big Black" Smith, lived in New York City. The media there had covered the lawsuit and the settlement extensively. Those downstate legislators knew little of us.

Gary Horton and I had become staunch advocates for organization and preparation, and we made sure that our members would not be ill-prepared as they ventured into the offices of legislators. I had readied "talking points" memoranda detailing the motivation behind our demands. With the sun rising along the Thruway, our members read and reread the handouts, like students prepping for exams. The drive to Albany was largely quiet, perhaps an indication of the seriousness of our mission. Or perhaps it was the early hour. Or both.

I had been chosen to be one of the speakers at the news conference, which opened one day before our lobbying session. We were squeezed into a small pressroom with five or six media members there. There was a sense that the Quinn family story—the murder by inmates of my father, the lack of concern and recompense from the state for my mother—was easier to tell than some others. I was also finding my voice within the FVOA. Once wary of the group meetings, I had become someone insistent that we be heard.

Still, I could not help but feel my emotions welling inside me as I told the gathered media of the loss of my father and its impact on me. My voice quavering, I told them, "My father was stolen from us. He missed our growing up. He missed our marriages. He has missed his grandchildren."

Ann D'Arcangelo Driscoll was pointed and direct as she told about how the state abandoned and deceived widows like her. "We were pushed under the rug," she said. "We were lied to. We were scammed." Ann was then working as a supervising nurse for the state corrections department, but she would not let her employment deter her from the truths of how she was treated.

Ann had long battled her own guilt about Attica. Before the uprising, there had been another riot at the Auburn Correctional Facility in central New York. Some inmates were transferred from there to Attica afterward. John Hill was in fact one of them.

When her husband was planning a transfer, Ann encouraged him to avoid Auburn because of the history. Attica was virtually "riot-proof," she and her husband had been told. He went there instead.

When Ann years later took a job as a nurse within the prison system, she was in a training session with a prison chaplain. The chaplain warned the new staff about speaking to the media. He showed a film clip of a young woman, whose husband was a hostage at Attica, speaking to the press during the standoff before the retaking.

"This woman got her husband killed," the chaplain said.

Ann was the woman on the film clip. Shaken, she raised her hand and corrected the chaplain. "The State Police killed her husband," she told him.

Ann would tell of moments like that. "Once again, the guilt set in," she once said. "Not only did I beg John to transfer to the riot-proof prison, now I am being told I caused his death."

At the Albany press conference, we fielded questions about why FVOA would refuse the $50,000 payments from the state and believed we deserved more. Some in the media were unaware of the court award to Lynda Jones from years before; we explained how that was our barometer for our restitution demand.

We also highlighted our other demands—funded counseling, an opening of records, the guaranteed annual ceremony, an apology from the state—and why these were also key to us. While we had local media coverage in western New York, this was the first opportunity in which we would likely get statewide coverage. The Associated Press was there to cover the news conference, and its story would surely go into New York newspapers, television, and radio stations, if not beyond.

We felt the news conference was a success, and we hoped it would generate public support for us. Next on the agenda was an equally important task—meetings with legislators.

My mother and I were assigned some of the more influential legislators, including Buffalo-based Assemblyman Arthur Eve.

I was nervous. Not only was I embarking on a lobbying campaign completely foreign to me, but I also knew that Eve had personal connections to the riot.

Eve had first been elected to the Assembly in 1966 and was known as a powerful supporter of liberal causes. He'd ascended to leadership positions throughout his Assembly career. He once threatened to lie down in front of bulldozers at a public-funded project because its plan didn't include minority-owned businesses as contractors. Former New York Governor Mario Cuomo once said of Eve, "Art is constantly reminding you that there are more people in pain, more who haven't had opportunity, more that needs to be done. He's a constant goad."

Eve had been among the civilians who tried to negotiate a settlement with the Attica inmates before the retaking by State Police. He had been the first "observer," as they were called, to enter Attica and listen to demands from the prisoners. The inmates had requested mediators whom they respected, and Eve was one. Others would join with him, including *New York Times* columnist Tom Wicker and fiery civil rights lawyer William Kunstler.

Eve was the first Dominican American elected to public office in the United States and was the first African American to win the Buffalo Mayoral Democratic primary, though he lost the mayoral election. His personal history concerned me. Eve was long seen as an ally of the inmates, and I was unsure just how he would receive us. My mother also knew the name of Arthur Eve. She knew he'd been an observer and that he had been at Attica because inmates trusted him. We did not know much more about Arthur Eve beyond the fact that he, like other observers, was chosen by prisoners to try to mediate their demands with corrections and state officials. This made us unsure whether we could count on his support. Because of his close ties with inmates during the uprising, we did not expect him to be an ally with our organization.

We could not have been more wrong.

He was our first scheduled meeting, and he, and not a staff member, answered the door to his office. With his graying moustache and goatee, there was a quiet dignity to Arthur Eve. He showed us kindness and respect, especially for my mother, from the very beginning. It was evident that he was there to listen to us, to sincerely listen to us.

Our Lobbying Begins

I don't think my mother imagined that she would ever be in the office of Arthur Eve, and here he was, hearing us out and intently listening to what we had to say.

With other legislators, our meetings would be more formal—listening to our demands squeezed in between meetings of many organizations making their own pitches for financial or legislative consideration. We knew that groups from human service nonprofits to animal shelters had their own hopes for legislative help, and some lawmakers might not distinguish between us and them.

But Arthur Eve knew Attica better than most. He knew what had happened there. He had tried his damnedest to stave off the violence that happened, and he forever, as I would learn, was haunted by a sense that he had failed. He should never have been burdened with a belief that he shouldered some responsibility for the deaths there, yet he was.

Arthur Eve wears his emotions on his sleeve, and we talked honestly and painfully of Attica. He was measured in what he said, not out of some fear that he would misspeak but more, I could tell, that he wanted every word to count. His integrity was obvious, his concern for us touching.

Remembering September 13, 1971, he told me, "I just didn't think they were going to come in shooting."

As we talked, I had a very difficult time keeping it together. I was ready for some mild obstructionist response to our demands from lawmakers, or some feigned concern that would not translate into legislative support. But here was Arthur Eve, one of the state's most powerful legislators, listening to us and hearing us.

He was apologetic to us; so few, as I would learn, would ever be apologetic to us. Yet here was a man who really had no cause to apologize to us, doing so.

This would not be my first meeting with Arthur Eve. He would become an essential friend to FVOA and a man whom I could call at any time of the day or night. To this day I keep voicemail messages from him that I refuse to erase. Among them: "Deanne Quinn Miller. This is Arthur O. Eve. I just want to wish you and your family a blessed and Merry Christmas. I just want you to know that I think of you."

My mother and I left the meeting with Arthur Eve feeling optimistic, with Mom being especially moved by the care he showed for her.

We met other key lawmakers that day, among them state Senator Michael Nozzolio, a western New York legislator who headed the Senate corrections committee, and Senator Dale Volker. As I would learn, Volker had his own take on what had happened at Attica, and he refused to see fault with the state's actions at the prison. Volker would also become key to FVOA negotiations, but he and I would never have the same relationship or the same trust that I would have with Arthur Eve. This was odd in some ways: Volker was a "law and order" Republican and Eve a liberal Democrat. Volker might seem the natural ally, but instead it was Arthur Eve who was most willing to help us. After all, Eve had witnessed the horrors of Attica firsthand.

At day's end, we returned to the bus for the trip home. Gary ensured that we were not done. He asked each group that had met with legislators to discuss how the session had gone. Some had met with lawmakers; others had been left with staff members. Gary also had us write out our thoughts on the meetings and whether we felt there were lawmakers whom we could count on to help with our demands. We also planned "thank you" notes for all with whom we'd spoken.

The meetings with downstate lawmakers proved especially helpful, because they knew nothing of our plight beforehand. Many of the New York City-area legislators did not know who we were or what we were about. There appeared to be a belief that, before the settlement, the inmates had received nothing for their suffering and injuries, yet we'd been made whole. Some thought we had even been overcompensated through the years, a misimpression left to stand because so few of the FVOA members had ever spoken out about their treatment. But, once they learned how the families had struggled, the downstate lawmakers realized that we, too, were victims of Attica. We hoped that, when the time came, we could also count on them for support.

The trip to Albany had been a grueling day, so perhaps it was no surprise that some of us needed to let off steam. Kentt Monteleone was known to make a potent and tasty and smooth homemade hard cider. He had brought some along. Some of the younger members gathered at the back of the bus, almost like a high school outing with class clowns and pranksters heading to the rear. They started sampling the product. The more drink was imbibed, the louder the rear of the bus got. There were occasionally curse words mixed in with the joking lightheartedness.

The widows were at the front of the bus; they were not pleased. They told us that this behavior would have to be discussed at our next meeting.

We promised that it would. It wasn't.

Instead, our meeting focused on our plans for more lobbying. There were more bus trips, more lawmakers to meet, and yes, more hard cider for the return trips. For some of our members, that cider would be a well-deserved treat after very long days—and we had many of them ahead.

CHAPTER NINE.

He Was Like
a Guardian Angel

A s we increased our outreach to lawmakers, the inmates were in the midst of their testimony in federal court before Judge Telesca in Rochester. These testimonies were open to the public, and anyone could attend. Members of the Forgotten Victims of Attica were split on the issue of attending. Some wanted nothing to do with the testimony while others, including the children of one of the slain hostages, did go to the hearings to hear what the inmates had to say.

I couldn't bring myself to go. I still didn't feel emotionally strong enough. But I had developed a sympathy for the inmates, hearing of the horrors they'd endured in the retaking. How do you hear stories of men treated as the prisoners were and think, "They were inmates. They deserved to be killed and beaten. They didn't deserve medical care." Their stories of abuse were horrific.

The Rochester daily newspaper, the *Democrat and Chronicle*, carried reports on the hearings, and I regularly consumed those stories. The newspaper's federal courts and investigative reporter (and this book's co-author), Gary Craig, had written of the settlement in January 2000.

He continued to follow the hearings, often alerted in advance by Judge Telesca as to what could be compelling and revealing testimony.

In mid-July, Craig wrote a story that focused on the testimony of Attica inmate Gene Hitchens. Headlined "Attica Testimony Shows a Soft Side," the piece highlighted in larger text a quote from Hitchens. "He was like a guardian angel," Hitchens said of a corrections officer at Attica. "I truly believe I didn't suffer there because he was there."

The corrections officer was my father.

Hitchens recalled how he was all of five-foot-two and could have been targeted by predatory inmates in the prison. Baby-faced and slight, Hitchens was jailed for a relatively minor forgery crime. Though a maximum security prison, Attica also housed some inmates with lesser crimes. Hitchens was one of those, and he wondered whether he'd been shipped to Attica by a judge to "scare him straight" from a life of crime. He'd dropped out of school in the ninth grade but did manage to secure a high school equivalency degree at Attica.

My father saw how treacherous life could be for the young man. Hitchens was twenty-two when at Attica—and my father would visit him to ensure he was not being victimized.

"It was like he'd check on me," Hitchens said. My father would ask him of his classes, how he was managing day-to-day in the prison.

"I felt safe because of that," Hitchens said. "I never felt like I was in danger until the riot."

"He was like a guardian angel," Hitchens said of my father. "He was good people. I truly believe I didn't suffer there because he was there and I wanted his family to know that."

Hitchens was not even in the Yard during the retaking. He'd been locked in a cell by corrections officers during the inmate uprising. This meant Hitchens was not eligible for restitution. He was not among the inmates who sued state and corrections officials in 1975.

Yet he'd flown from Miami, Florida, on his own dime to testify in front of Telesca. Yes, he said, he wanted to purge the demons of Attica that for years had haunted him. But, mostly, he wanted the family of William Quinn to know what kind of man my father was.

"If anybody associated with Officer Quinn is in this courtroom today, I am so terribly sorry that that man lost his life," Hitchens said in court. "That man looked after me and I felt safe because of him and, I guess, I was able to hold on to my humanity because of his concern for me."

I was not in the court, but after reading the article I knew I wanted to speak with Gene Hitchens. I realized that he had information that I desperately needed to know.

I knew little about my father on the job. My father lived a life of twenty-eight years—almost twenty-two of them without me—and he had this whole life that I didn't know because no one shared it with me. And here was a man—a former prisoner, of all people—who could tell me more of my dad.

From the stories I had heard from friends, and the ones my family had sparingly told me, I sensed my father was a good man, a decent man, a man who wanted to do right. I knew that he had a degree in criminal justice. I knew that he had once worked with children with disabilities. All of this pointed to a man who wanted to help others.

Still, I did not know what he was like as a corrections officer. I did not know if he saw inmates as human beings or, as some on the job did, as lesser than human.

On the July day when I read the article, I telephoned Gary Craig at the *Democrat and Chronicle* and asked whether he could connect me with Hitchens. Craig passed on Hitchens's telephone number, which he'd gotten from the former inmate while interviewing him after his testimony. I called Hitchens right away.

He Was Like a Guardian Angel

That conversation would be the first of several with Hitchens. And we also wrote to each other occasionally. Through our talks and letters, I learned not only more of my father but of Hitchens, as well.

He'd fallen into drugs at an early age, and a series of minor crimes followed. He'd stolen from family and friends to support his habit. He'd tried treatment programs, but none had worked when he was young.

He landed at Attica and kept to himself there to avoid trouble. He focused on the education the corrections system provided, securing his GED within six months at the prison. He described himself as "a little kid in a prison of giants."

When the riot erupted, he did not have much time left on his sentence. But the riot scarred him for years to come. Later, when the testimony of the inmate hearings became public, I received a copy and read what Hitchens had said in full in Telesca's courtroom. He'd spoken of the riot's impact on him and how it derailed him and his efforts to stabilize his life after incarceration.

Hitchens was in the prison's Times Square when he saw the onslaught of fellow inmates coming toward him on September 9, 1971.

"I never felt like I was in danger until the riot," he said in court. "The morning of the riot was the first time I was afraid of Attica. I felt helpless and I felt like I didn't have people looking after me. I thought although I was a junkie and had committed enough crimes to be locked up, I still felt like I should have been safe at Attica.

"On...the day of the riot I lost that feeling. I was at Times Square and just the world came apart. It fell apart."

Some corrections officers whom Hitchens did not know grabbed him, essentially using him as a shield. "They didn't know me like Officer Quinn," Hitchens said. "To the other officers I guess I was just a louse. That's how it looked, like I was a louse and running loose and I was part of this other band of inmates, a louse."

The officers dragged him up and down stairs, injuring his arm in the process before locking him in a cell. He spent the next four days there and witnessed the retaking through a cell window. An officer came into his cell and forced him to watch the bloody mayhem, Hitchens said.

It seemed "like hours" as the clouds of tear gas fell and the staccato gunfire continued, Hitchens said. He saw prisoners, their hands in the air, shot in what he considered heartless homicides. The images would never leave him.

"What do you do with that?" Hitchens told Judge Telesca. "What do you do with that?"

Here was another Attica victim with his own emotional trauma. The riot had damaged so many, its ripples of heartache never ceasing to expand.

For Hitchens, the appearance in Rochester was not only an opportunity to remind the world of the character of my father but an attempt at closure. After the riot, he bounced in and out of prisons in Connecticut and Florida for sixteen years before finally stepping away from crime. He engaged in serious and intense therapy for several years, trying to rid himself of the violent images that he'd seen through the prison window bars.

In 1994 he was even selected as a finalist for a Kellogg Foundation Fellowship in a program that tries to build leadership from a diverse class of applicants. As he recalled in the Rochester courtroom, the interview was proceeding well, and then he was asked about Attica. He found himself immobilized, unable to speak about what he'd witnessed or its impact on him.

"They asked me out of nowhere about Attica and I couldn't complete the interview because of it," he said. "And then I realized I had not dealt with Attica. So, I didn't get the fellowship, but I went back into therapy and it's been a better life for me since. It was then that I decided that I wasn't going to wear Attica on my sleeves, punish society, blame anybody for my misfortunes, whatever happened in my past."

He had succeeded in building a career in Miami, working as an ombudsman for battered women and helping them secure public assistance. "I want to make a contribution," he told Telesca. "I want to give to my community in big ways."

In court, Hitchens said he'd felt slighted by Frank "Big Black" Smith, who, as one of the lead defendants in the case, was in the courtroom each day. Smith worked closely with attorney Elizabeth Fink; he'd become a paralegal after his incarceration. He organized inmate testimony, helping arrange bus trips to Rochester with former prisoners who lived in the New York City region.

Before Hitchens's testimony, Smith hugged many of the former inmates who'd trekked from downstate New York. He did not hug Hitchens. Near the end of his testimony, with his voice shaking, Hitchens said to Smith, "You didn't hug me, man, because I guess I wasn't in the Yard. . . . I wasn't there. Didn't nothing happen to me."

Smith explained that he had not recognized Hitchens and did not know him since he had not come with the group of former inmates who had traveled by bus.

"Man, I would have been glad to give you a hug," Smith said. "I just didn't know who you were. I love you, man, I love you. God bless."

I was not in the courtroom for that moment, but it was clear from the transcript testimony that Hitchens wanted to release himself from Attica forever. But he also wanted an acknowledgment that he was as much of a survivor as anyone, even if he had not been in the Yard.

"I'm leaving Attica here today, your honor. This is where Attica ends for me. I'm not dragging it. . . . I don't want to live it again."

In our telephone conversations in the days and weeks later, I, too, sensed that Hitchens longed to leave the riot behind. He had been kind enough to tell me of my father, and to fly to Rochester to testify about the humanity of my father. I could never forget that.

But I also did not want him to revisit a part of his life that he longed to escape. Our phone calls stopped, as did our letters.

Gene Hitchens was moving on from Attica. Perhaps I should have envied him for that. But my journey was largely just beginning. There was so much more to know about my father and about the riot.

And I now recognized that I could not only learn from the men who were my father's colleagues but also from the men who had been imprisoned at Attica when my father worked there.

Gene Hitchens taught me that.

CHAPTER TEN

The Guard Who Survived

A mong those who decided to testify before Judge Telesca at the Rochester Federal Court hearing was a man who had not been an inmate at the time of the riot. In fact, he'd been a corrections officer.

That man was Michael Smith.

Michael had testified at the earlier inmate civil trial in Buffalo, and Elizabeth Fink asked him to testify again in Rochester. Judge Telesca could have opted not to allow Michael to testify, but he instead wanted to hear what the hostage who nearly died had to say.

Michael didn't hesitate to accept Fink's invitation. Some in our group might have been upset to see Michael testifying at the inmate settlement, but by this time they knew better than to challenge Michael's choices. He has always been true to himself, and he believed that his testimony could help others and also allow him to again confront the state's version of Attica. He knew about the conditions in the prison that sparked the riot. He knew that the retaking was ill-advised; he almost didn't survive. And, as Michael would tell Judge Telesca, just as he had told others through the years, he believed he was saved by an inmate.

Michael was assigned to the second-floor metal shop on September 9, 1971, when, as he said in court, he heard "inmates trying to break through the door downstairs." They succeeded. "This wave of human emotion exploded into the room where I was," he said. "I was struck and knocked to the floor, and I was being beaten."

Two inmates he knew then lay spread-eagled over Michael to protect him. They told "the other inmates that I was a good guy and to leave me alone," he said.

One of the inmates who helped Michael was Don Noble, the same prisoner who months before had asked him to review the letter outlining prisoner demands for better conditions. The demands were not outrageous, Michael said.

"That list grew with time, but initially all the demands were of a humanitarian nature and very understandable concerns," Michael said in court.

Michael stressed the particularly volatile times in 1971. The anti-war efforts were still in full bloom, and civil rights protests were common across the country. Those movements, which some considered radical, had made their way into the prisons. Inmates, especially Black and Latino prisoners, were fighting for basic human rights. That's why Noble had, months before the riot, shown Michael the list of inmate demands. Michael had treated Noble and other inmates with decency; in turn, they respected his opinions.

"I reviewed [the list]," Michael said, remembering what Noble had shown him, "and told him that in my honest opinion there wasn't anything there that I thought was out of order and it was well put together and addressed issues that should be addressed."

On September 9, Noble was unable to get Michael out of the prison, but he did take him to the D Yard where Michael joined the growing number of hostages. By the time the riot had calmed, the inmates were holding forty-two prison employees captive, men they hoped to use as bargaining chips.

The Guard Who Survived

In the Yard, Michael said, the Muslim inmates ensured he and other hostages were safe. He remembered "hearing one of the Muslim leaders instructing one of their men that if anyone tries to break through their perimeter to kill them or die protecting the hostages."

For the first days, he and other hostages and inmates believed there was progress being made with negotiations. Then word came that my father had died on September 11, and that changed everything. Inmates began to emphasize the need for amnesty because, otherwise, some would surely be prosecuted for the murder of my father.

Amnesty was unlikely, especially since a New York criminal statute could have held most, if not all, of the rioters responsible for my father's death. On the day of my father's death, District Attorney Louis James of Wyoming County, where the prison is located, said he could not and would not agree to any amnesty for riot-related crimes. He did place in writing that he would prosecute "only when in my judgment there is substantial evidence to link a specific individual with the commission of a specific crime."

Some of the citizen "observers"—reporters, civil rights leaders, and others whom the inmates had selected as negotiators during the stand-off—took this as a victory. But it did not ensure that the rioting masses couldn't be prosecuted for the murder of William Quinn. A felony murder charge is allowed if a victim is killed during the commission of a separate felony, such as the riot. The prosecutor's agreement did not fully address that fact and did not completely close the door on widespread prosecutions for my father's death.

I've often wondered whether things would have turned out differently if authorities told the inmates that only those who could be directly tied to my father's death, as Hill and Pernasilice later were, would be prosecuted. What if the inmates knew that only those who beat my father would be accused of assault or murder? Could that have saved the thirty-nine men who died on September 13?

Criminal amnesty would not be given. That realization encouraged the inmates to push for an absurd demand—a request that they be transported to a "non-imperialistic country." So many of the inmate demands made sense—sanitary conditions, life-changing educational opportunities, religious freedom—and now, with tensions nearing a breaking point, the demands went from the possible to the impossible.

Testifying before Telesca in 2000, Michael told how my father's death changed the mood within the Attica walls.

"I had been fairly optimistic as I think a lot of the hostages were up until that point, and then the negotiation process went south from there. It seemed to break down," Michael said.

On Sunday night, September 12, Michael got an ink pen from an inmate and, on business cards and dollar bills in his wallet, wrote a goodbye note to his wife, Sharon, and his family. He hoped it would be found should he die. This was so typical of Michael, to have the wherewithal and strength to do that. I have never heard of anything so heartbreaking or desperate. I cannot imagine his thoughts as he penned what he suspected would be his final words to his loved ones. That night, a priest was sent into the Yard to administer last rites to the hostages.

The next morning, Michael was taken, blindfolded, to the prison catwalk. He had three men assigned as "executioners." The inmates were trying to pressure the state officials and police gathered outside the prison into an acceptance of all demands. They also hoped to head off an assault.

They failed on both measures.

One of Michael's executioners was Don Noble. Michael and Noble talked of how their lives could end on the catwalk. Noble asked Michael, if he survived, to find his family and tell them he loved them. Michael asked the same from Noble and told him, "When the time comes, Don, I want you to make it quick as possible. I don't want to suffer."

The Guard Who Survived

Michael had relived the moments that came next a number of times before that day in the Rochester courtroom. He had testified at trial about it; he had told his story to movie producers who made an HBO film about Attica; and he had talked among FVOA members. And again Michael, with the same precision and thoughtful pauses as when I first heard him speak, recounted what could have been his final minutes on the planet.

Michael was seated on a chair on the catwalk, with Noble to his left, when the helicopters rose above the Attica prison walls. He remembered "the concussion of the propellers above me," and, though still blind-folded, he knew from the smell and the growing cacophony of shouts from the inmates that tear gas had been dropped into the prison.

Then the gunfire began.

"I spent a lot of time hunting in my youth and I can recall sitting there and being able to identify the types of weapons that were being fired, and it was unbelievable. There were shotguns. There were large-caliber hand-guns. There were small-caliber handguns. There were semi-automatic weapons. There were automatic weapons."

Michael would later see a film made by State Police during the retaking that showed what happened next. One inmate to Michael's side wielded a homemade spear and was ready to drive it into Michael's chest. Suddenly, the man was shot. Don Noble then tugged at Michael, and Michael lowered his body, just as the inmate behind him was shot. Michael pushed up his blindfold, just as he and Noble were leveled by gunfire.

"We fell like dominoes. The fellow with the spear went over the railing."

Michael described his wounds, saying that whoever shot him was an excellent marksman. He has long wondered how he was shot so precisely, with four shots entering just below his navel.

He recalled lying on the catwalk as the shooting continued. "Chips of cement and bullets were hitting all around me. You could hear people crying and people dying and people screaming."

When the shooting stopped, a state trooper approached Michael and aimed a shotgun at his head. "I thought, 'I made it this far and now he's going to blow my head off.'"

A corrections officer saw Michael and told the trooper who he was. The trooper pointed the shotgun at Noble. "Don't shoot," Michael said. "His name is Don Noble, and he saved my life." The trooper moved on.

For the inmates and attorney Elizabeth Fink, Michael's testimony reinforced how the abysmal conditions at the prison were the seeds of the riot and how the retaking seemed an unplanned recipe for disaster and death. And what could not be forgotten was that one of the law enforcement officers who was among the police ranks seizing control of the prison had seemed perfectly ready to mistake Michael for an inmate and shoot him in the face.

"It was a bungled mess," Michael said of the retaking. "I don't have any animosity towards the inmates. I wouldn't have wanted the job that the troopers had [with the retaking]. People on both sides made mistakes. People on both sides did things they shouldn't have done, and both sides should have been held responsible for their actions, and especially New York State."

Months before his testimony, I had first heard Michael Smith at the Signature Café, and I felt then that he carried with him some truths that I needed to hear. Even as I followed the testimony through the media, including coverage of Michael's testimony, I still could not bring myself to attend the hearings.

I have since read his testimony from Judge Telesca's court, and I will never forget what he said toward the end.

"Bill Quinn," Michael said, and I can almost hear the pause that came then.

"Bill Quinn's family never got any—they never got any closure."

With a photograph of my late father, William Quinn. CREDIT: *Democrat and Chronicle*, Shawn Dowd

My parents' wedding day, May 1, 1965, at St. Vincent's Church in Attica, New York. CREDIT: Deanne Quinn Miller

My maternal grandparents, Ferris and Eunice Willard, on my parent's wedding day, May 1, 1965. My grandparents' wedding anniversary was the next day, May 2. CREDIT: Deanne Quinn Miller

Family vacation photo at Cayuga Lake
CREDIT: Deanne Quinn Miller

Dad, Christine, me, and our dog Charlie. Picture taken at our house in Attica on Windsor Street. CREDIT: Deanne Quinn Miller

Easter photo taken on the steps of my grandfather and grandmother Quinn's house on 75 East Avenue. Christine was six months old, I was two-and-a-half. CREDIT: Deanne Quinn Miller

Our bedtime routine: Dad reading to Christine and me in our home on Windsor Street. CREDIT: Deanne Quinn Miller

Visit to my godmother's house in Wilmington, Delaware, in June 1971. I was five and Christine was three. CREDIT: Deanne Quinn Miller

This photo of us was taken at Grandpa and Grandma Willard's house. Our new baby sister Amy was about a month old, pictured here with Christine and me. CREDIT: Deanne Quinn Miller

Christine, myself, and our beloved Labrador Charlie at my Grandpa and Grandma Willard's house, summer of 1972. Our dresses were made by our grandmother Quinn. CREDIT: Deanne Quinn Miller

My dad's New York State gun permit ID photo. CREDIT: Deanne Quinn Miller

An honor guard of 400 correction officers and firemen from all over the state led the funeral procession through downtown Attica for my father, William Quinn, killed during the prison riot. CREDIT: Bill Ray/The LIFE Picture Collection via Getty Images

The crowd outside the funeral service for my father, William Quinn. CREDIT: *Democrat and Chronicle*

CHAPTER ELEVEN

Big Black and I

There is one moment during Michael Smith's testimony that is not revealed by the court transcripts from June 20, 2000. Michael was the hostage who, in 1971, had allegedly been castrated by inmate Frank "Big Black" Smith. But that allegation, circulated by State Police and some corrections officials after the retaking, was a complete lie.

The transcript reads: "Before I was out of the prison, state officials... reported to the Associated Press that I had been castrated by Frank Smith and my testicles stuffed in my mouth. It never happened. I was never assaulted. With the exception of the very first initial day in the metal shop, I was never assaulted in any way."

The transcripts do not tell what happened elsewhere in the courtroom during this testimony. But Rochester *Democrat and Chronicle* reporter Gary Craig was there, and he wrote, "As Michael Smith yesterday told Telesca there was no truth to the claims of castration, Frank Smith wiped tears from his eyes, stood and left his seat in the courtroom."

For Frank Smith, Michael's testimony was particularly poignant. The malignant rumor had spread so quickly and so powerfully that it unleashed the wrath of the men who stormed the prison and rounded up inmates.

Because of that rumor, Frank "Big Black" Smith was tortured.

I had heard some of Frank's story before but usually only in news snippets from the Buffalo civil trial from years before. His life was rarely detailed in the news coverage.

Frank's mother, the daughter of a former slave, was a cotton picker in South Carolina before she moved her family to Brooklyn when Frank was only five years old. Like Gene Hitchens, he fell into drugs when young. He was smoking marijuana and using cocaine as a teenager.

Frank found himself occasionally in trouble with the law. He had arrived at Attica in 1965 on a conviction for an armed robbery of a craps game.

At the prison, he befriended inmates and corrections officers alike. After the initial chaos of the riot, he was a popular choice to head the security team that would protect the men taken hostage. He reached out to Muslim inmates to help him.

In his testimony to Telesca, Frank described the "blood and violence" of the retaking, with men—inmates and hostages alike—falling dead around him.

"Then, your Honor, I started hearing my name being called. "Where's Big Black? Where's Big Black?"

Frank at first thought he was being sought out because he had tried to maintain the peace. He had helped escort the civilian negotiators in and out of the prison, making sure they stayed safe. But, instead, he was being targeted for retaliation. The first corrections officer who found him beat him with a baton.

Stripped naked, Frank was then forced to lie upon a table. Corrections officers and state troopers surrounded him, placing a football under his throat. They dropped burning cigarettes on him, promising he would be killed if he released the football.

Frank heard the claims from his torturers that he'd castrated a hostage; he had no idea where the rumor had come from. He simply knew it was not true.

"After laying on the table for four, five hours, being threatened and being talked to about castration, [being] poked, burned, trying to move my body so I could get the cigarettes off me, trying to fight myself to keep from getting off the table...I just felt a lot of times that it would be better just to go on and let them kill me."

Finally freed from the table, Frank walked barefoot through the fragments of broken glass as he was beaten mercilessly with batons. His wrists were broken, his head split open. He fell unconscious and was taken to a medical room, only to awaken with a member of the State Police standing over him, aiming a shotgun at his head.

"Open your eyes, nigger," he said. "We're going to kill you just like you cut that officer's nuts off."

He was finally released to his cell, where officers threatened to shoot him. And he was beaten again.

Frank Smith was the first inmate to testify before Telesca, and, as I would learn following the hearings from afar, he helped organize all of the subsequent testimony from inmates. He also ensured that the inmates submitted their written claims. What I didn't know then, and would later learn, was that Frank and Judge Telesca were developing a deep friendship.

During that same summer of 2000, as inmate testimony continued, the Forgotten Victims of Attica efforts were gaining momentum. We held fundraisers; we continued to lobby lawmakers; our press coverage expanded from simply regional attention to statewide media interest.

I took on a serious organizational role. I wrote letters for FVOA, signing my name. I looked up legal statutes for Gary and Jonathan Gradess, who was becoming a key supporter for us in Albany. I became the go-to media contact. I was working daily for FVOA; it became a twenty-hour a week job, at least. In many ways, the work I was doing with FVOA was similar to the paralegal work Frank Smith was doing shepherding the inmate testimony.

I'd occasionally talk to Gary about Frank, and Gary encouraged me to reach out to him. I could not bring myself to do that at first. I also was talking to *Democrat and Chronicle* reporter Gary Craig more now; in addition to the inmate settlement and testimony, he was now writing about FVOA. He also suggested that I talk to Frank and, as with Gene Hitchens, passed on his phone number. All who recommended that I call Frank told me that he was a special and caring individual who likely would welcome the contact.

For weeks I kept the telephone number, finding reasons not to call. Some evenings I would be on the verge of calling, then decide it was too late. Or I would imagine that Frank was eating dinner and I did not want to interrupt. It was a hesitancy driven by fear of rejection, to be honest. What if he did not welcome a call from me? I was unsure just how I would react. What if he declined to answer the questions that I desperately wanted to ask?

At the same time, I knew that Frank Smith, as a central figure in the history of the uprising, could tell me more about those tragic 1971 days than could others. And he had a perspective that no one else did. He had been subjected to unfathomable abuse yet had come out the other side. He would not let the state forget what had happened to him, but he also had not let it destroy his spirit—at least from what I had read and heard of the man.

So, finally, I called.

From the first minutes of the call, Frank did what he could to shake my fears and settle my nerves. He knew of my work with FVOA, and he said, "I hoped there'd be a time when you and I could talk." He had the same baritone voice that I'd heard in television interviews. It was laced with warmth. Somehow, Frank Smith could set you at ease, and he did just that with me during the telephone call. There was just such a comfort talking with him, and we would talk many more times.

On our first telephone call, he did most of the talking. And he was so funny in the conversation. He said, "Girl, you can ask me anything. I know you've probably got questions. And I've got answers. I'm an open book and you can ask me whatever you want to ask me." To this day, I still find it remarkable that someone could endure what he did and still want to take a call from me, a prison guard's daughter.

That call began the first of what would be weekly or biweekly Sunday night phone calls. After the first call, he said, "We can talk next week if you want to." At first, I worried about boundaries with him. But he made sure that I knew I could ask him anything.

In one of our first conversations, I asked him about the security detail. I wondered whether they were there to truly protect the hostages. I wondered whether the hostages were kept blindfolded in a circle to make it easier to kill them should the time come. I felt bad asking, knowing that it came from my mistrust of some of the inmates. But he made clear that his intention was to keep the hostages safe.

He did not balk at all when asked that particular question or any others I had. On Sunday nights I would go to a downstairs office in our home and call Frank at 7 p.m. Nothing was off-limits in our conversations. He knew my father and grandfather, who'd been a meat cutter at the prison, and he liked both of them. He told me his story of how he wound up as a prisoner in Attica, and we talked about the turmoil in the months that led up to the riot. He spoke about the conditions, the inhumane way some corrections officers treated inmates, his days in the Yard before the retaking.

I could ask him even about nagging details about the history of the riot that bothered me, and he would always answer as best as he could.

Frank and I developed a very intense emotional connection, finding that many of our views on the riot were surprisingly similar. He was kind, compassionate, and truthful. We exchanged stories of our lives and how we lived in the aftermath of Attica. We had a connection that only those who lived through Attica could understand, regardless of what "side" you were on. Frank, too, knew that there were many grave injustices that had happened at Attica.

There were several moments on the phone when all we could hear were each other's sobs, as we talked of particularly painful times in our lives. Sometimes I would finish the phone call, eyes red from crying, and my husband would ask if I was okay. And I was. I was finding something in my regular talks with Frank that I had not found elsewhere when confronting Attica.

There were times when Frank would say, "Do you mind if I ask you this?" and he would then ask about how the state handled the deaths of our family members. I told him of the sometimes heartless way the state had told families of the deaths of their loved ones and that the state paid for funerals, while including that compensation as another legal barrier to a lawsuit. Like the workers' compensation, the state contended that the widows had opted for state assistance as another legal "election of remedy."

Frank just couldn't believe it. He thought the families were "being taken care of" with some kind of substantial financial amends. Apparently, that's what many inmates thought, as well.

And we didn't just talk about Attica. Instead, we often talked just as close friends would. He'd inquire about our daughters, joking and asking if they were giving us problems. He'd talk about the work he was doing, mentoring youth at a recreation center. He said he did not want them to travel his path, and I assured him that he'd turned out a remarkably special person. "I wish I'd gotten here another way," he said.

Early on, he encouraged me to call him "Black" instead of "Frank." That was what he preferred. I felt uncomfortable with the nickname at first; it seemed wrong coming from me. But it soon became second nature.

Big Black and I

It was also early on when Frank dubbed me "Little White." He said, "I'm Big Black and you're Little White." It was hysterical. And Frank had this wonderful, booming laugh. He'd often make himself crack up in the middle of some story he was telling. That laugh was the definition of joy.

We also talked about the similarity of our roles—mine with the FVOA and his as the paralegal organizing inmate testimony. We both had individuals causing us problems, and we joked about the challenges of working with those folks.

Each of our groups had members who greatly distrusted the state. Frank had tried to calm inmates who thought there would be no settlement money and that the state was instead trying to trick them by gathering their testimony to somehow use against them.

But there was one topic I would not ask him about, and that was his torture. I didn't feel it appropriate at all for me to ask him of that, or to expect him to relive it. I had read all I needed to know about it. I knew it was true; I knew it was unforgivable.

The talks continued, on and off, for several years. In 2003, Frank was stricken with kidney cancer. When I found out he was sick it hit me hard. There were days that were more difficult for him than others, and I could tell he was growing weaker in our conversations. But neither of us wanted those talks to end. Sometimes they were just short calls, to let him know I was thinking of him.

When I learned of his cancer, I bought a dozen cards of the "get well" variety and would send them to him in North Carolina, where he and his wife Pearl had moved. I mailed most of them, except two. Frank died in August 2004 before I could mail those last ones. I still have them. They were for Frank Smith. I can't send them to anybody else.

I never met Frank face-to-face. Judge Telesca had offered to arrange a meeting between us. But it never happened. Still, our phone calls were a connection unlike any other. I truly believe my life was made better by knowing Frank. We had both survived something atrocious, and he reminded me many times that I, too, was a victim of Attica.

It was Judge Telesca who said Frank had told him in their last conversation that there was "unfinished business" with Attica. The FVOA was still fighting for our demands at that time; Frank wanted the state to make us whole.

Frank even once wrote Governor Pataki, imploring him to provide restitution for our group. "It is only fair to compensate the hostages and the families who lost them," he wrote. "The hardship and pain they suffered can't be separated from the [inmates']."

As Judge Telesca told the *New York Times* in an obituary, "Frank had this ability to forgive."

CHAPTER TWELVE

Increasing the Pressure

At the start of the year 2000, I never would have imagined that by year's end I would have transformed from a woman longing yet fearful to learn more of the Attica uprising to one in a leadership role with a group like the Forgotten Victims of Attica. And I had never imagined that I would be talking to men like Frank "Big Black" Smith and Gene Hitchens and finding my life richer for it.

And then there were men like Gary and Jonathan, who clearly came from different political ideologies than common in my household and community. They took me down a different path than what I'd known my entire life. They challenged my thinking about inmates and, for that matter, the entire version of the riot that I had heard for so long.

And I was willing to consider the riot from multiple perspectives. My past reading about Attica, in high school and college, had enlightened me some about the conditions at the prison and the treatment of the prisoners there. But I was also still eager for information about the uprising, and I worried that if I stepped away from FVOA my learning would come to a stop.

There was another reason my role with FVOA became more prominent: As our lobbying continued, I quickly learned the power of my last name.

The name "Quinn" got me access—on the phone with and into the offices of lawmakers who otherwise might not have given me the time of day. When you speak of Bill Quinn and his murder, those who want to hold the inmates responsible for all of the death and destruction and suffering at Attica tend to listen. My father was killed by prisoners; the story is that simple. It is not as simple to try to explain why the state chose to chaotically overtake the prison on September 13, 1971, fatally shooting thirty-nine men. Or why inmates suffered such shameful beatings and brutality after the retaking.

"Law and order" legislators did not want to consider that their own police forces, as well as the corrections officials and high-ranking state politicians, shouldered some burden for the catastrophe that was the Attica riot and retaking. But they were willing to meet with me because they assumed I shared similar opinions. My name got me into places I otherwise would not have gotten into.

I struggled with this identity—my being "Bill Quinn's daughter." It wasn't that I wanted to run from the legacy of my father, but I'd spent so much of my youth being recognized mostly as the daughter of a slain prison guard. I'd wanted to carve out my own identity, even while thirsting for information about Attica. In my growing role with FVOA, I had to come to terms; the Quinn name was very powerful when we went to Albany to seek assistance from state legislators.

Still, neither my name nor the increasing public recognition of FVOA could alter the response of state lawmakers when we rebuffed the offer of $550,000 for the 11 widows who'd lost their husbands at Attica. The legislators apparently believed that we would accept the offer and that they could be done with us.

It had been a difficult decision for the widows. I talked to my mother about how important the $50,000 could be for her. But she, like the other widows, stayed firm. They knew others had suffered, and they decided that all must be compensated.

I'm surprised even now with the blowback we received. Some lawmakers who portrayed themselves as our most reliable supporters appeared to be the angriest. State Senator Dale Volker said that we were "making a mistake" for turning the offer down, and let it be known to some of our members, including myself.

Negotiations did not go easy, and small-town politics could occasionally rear its head. State Assemblyman Dan Burling had previously been a Genesee County legislator, and he did not always get along with Gary, the county's public defender. Gary was a vigilant warrior for his office and indigent clients. Dan Burling was not a fan, and that friction also found its way into negotiations, even though Gary simply acted as counsel and the group made all of its own decisions.

Looking back on our initial lobbying efforts, I see how naïve we were. We believed that the state would quickly recognize how we'd been mistreated and would take legislative steps to rectify that wrong. The families had been expected to survive on the pittance of workers' compensation payments; the corrections officers who survived Attica had to return to work with little thought about what they'd endured; and those same men were discouraged from talking with each other.

We expected that once these facts became commonly known, we would find attentive and sympathetic lawmakers and state officials. Instead, we encountered resistance, especially after we refused the state's restitution offer.

That resistance made us stronger. And it made me even more committed to our cause.

Even as some lawmakers thought of distancing themselves from our group, we were building ranks with powerful allies, most notably the union for corrections officers, the New York State Correctional Officers & Police Benevolent Association (NYSCOPBA).

The NYSCOPBA president, Rick Harcrow, had worked at Attica for years. It was there that he became a union steward in 1996, then advanced up the leadership ladder. Under him, NYSCOPBA became a politically powerful union which often seemed to have direct channels to the office of Governor George Pataki.

At Attica, Harcrow worked with corrections officers who'd lost loved ones and colleagues at Attica, including Mark and John Cunningham, whose father, Sgt. Edward Cunningham, was killed in the retaking. Mark Cunningham trained Harcrow and was often Harcrow's supervisor, sometimes having conversations about the riot. Rick's father had been a marine in the Korean War, shot twice during the Battle of Inchon, and Harcrow was sure his father occasionally battled post-traumatic stress disorder. His father would sometimes get together with his wartime buddies, drink into the wee hours of the morning, then weep as they recalled their experiences. Harcrow suspected that Attica survivors had their own PTSD, and he did not want them to relive September 1971.

Once FVOA became active, Harcrow learned how the families and survivors had been treated by the state. He, like others, had assumed New York had taken care of the families. Working with Mark Cunningham, Harcrow offered to help however he could. He also had connections with other corrections unions, including the deep-pocketed and powerful California Correctional Peace Officers Association (CCPOA). The California union has long-reaching political arms, and their members quickly became active supporters of FVOA.

Harcrow also thought the state had erred with its decision to storm the prison. How, he would often ask in conversations with lawmakers, had the state expected anything but mass casualties?

I started talking to Rick Harcrow regularly in the summer of 2000, especially after we'd rejected the state's offer. We became close friends, and, as I did with Frank, we'd sometimes engage in conversations that would become tearful. Rick, six-foot-tall and weighing 260 pounds, is secretly a "softy" with a heart as big as he is.

I leaned hard on Rick, and he was always there for us. He later told people that I was the perfect spokeswoman for FVOA and that he was moved by my tenacity and resilience. I didn't realize I was exhibiting those traits. I was just pushing toward a goal. Rick often told me that he used to see my number on his cell phone and he would hesitate to immediately answer, but he knew I'd keep calling until he answered.

Corrections officers and others in law enforcement are taught a technique called "multiple strike overload," meaning that, if assaulted, you should strike back with a series of blows to a single location while trying to restrain the assailant. Rick used what he considered a similar approach with lobbying; he would push and push and push the same officials—those who held power—and would not give up until they paid attention to his words and wishes.

Rick also brought the union's media strategist, Tom Butler, into the fold. The son of a longtime state assemblyman, Butler was so moved by our stories that he agreed to help with publicity at no cost to us or the union.

Butler saw the need for more expansive airing of the history of FVOA and our treatment by the state. He reached out to media contacts across the state and managed to get us on news shows in Albany and the down-state Hudson Valley area. As Butler would later say, the stories of the inmates and their families had been chronicled and told, but our history was left unspoken.

Throughout the rest of 2000, FVOA engaged in fundraising activities and continued to generate media coverage. Kentt Monteleone, the son of a deceased hostage, loved to ride his Harley and put together what became a FVOA "Ride for Justice." We'd have 100 to 150 riders from around the state and beyond. The ride ended at the Quality Work Life building with a barbecue where FVOA members would speak publicly to the crowd about our mission. It became a successful annual fundraising event.

There were also benefit concerts, T-shirt sales, belt buckles, and commemorative coins. The unions also stepped up, helping with some financing. Only months before, we had started at a small café in Attica, hearing each other's stories, and now we were becoming a truly strong lobbying force.

Even Frank Smith was going to bat for us. As Judge Telesca had said after Frank died, Frank was a man of immense forgiveness.

The Forgotten Victims of Attica was making headlines and headway, and the truth of Attica was emerging.

CHAPTER THIRTEEN

Meeting the Attica Prosecutor

I n the summer of 2000, Michael and Sharon Smith and surviving hostage John Stockholm and his wife Mary traveled to Vermont to visit one of Attica's most controversial figures, Malcolm Bell.

Bell had been tasked after the riot as a special prosecutor to oversee and coordinate the prosecution of State Police and other law enforcement who may have committed crimes, including murder, in the retaking of Attica. A Harvard law school graduate, he had previously been a corporate attorney; he had no criminal experience. He would later wonder if he'd been chosen for this very reason. The cases against inmates were being handled by an investigative team with criminal pedigree. Did the state want police prosecutions to be less dependable?

Whether true or not, Malcolm's prosecutions were derailed by Governor Hugh Carey's amnesty and pardon decree in December 1976. But, even before that, he came to believe that state and corrections officials at the highest level were trying to impede his investigations. While the state was aggressively pushing for the convictions of inmates, it appeared loath to admit that its police forces committed crimes—including wanton killings that could be characterized as murder—in the seizure of D Yard.

Some in our group had decided that Malcolm might be helpful for our cause. In 1975, he had gone to the *New York Times* with his belief that his investigations had been thwarted. The subsequent news coverage turned him into a significant whistleblower in the historical annals of the Attica riot. Some in FVOA decided that he had knowledge and insights that others did not, and he also could be a dynamic ally.

I wasn't one of them.

It wasn't that I didn't know Malcolm's whistleblowing history. I did. I wasn't bothered by that. But Malcolm had once provided a legal affidavit saying that John Hill should be released from prison.

After Governor Carey's 1976 action, the state Parole Board kept Hill in prison. It kept finding ways to ensure he was not released, denying him parole for the crimes that originally landed him at Attica. It was clear that the Parole Board's decisions were driven by the conviction of Hill for the murder of my father, even though Hill's prison sentence for the killing had been set aside by the gubernatorial commutation—the only commutation for the murdering of a peace officer in judicial history at that time. In one ruling, the Parole Board said that the release of Hill could "cause a widespread negative community reaction and would probably promote disrespect for the law."

Hill's lawyer, William Kunstler, sought out Malcolm for his opinion on whether Hill should be released, and Malcolm provided the affidavit saying that Hill should be treated as all other inmates who had faced criminal charges or had been convicted of Attica-related crimes. It was unfair to keep him jailed after Carey's decrees, Malcolm concluded.

I knew of Malcolm Bell's efforts on Hill's behalf—and I was not happy with what he'd done. I didn't like the commutation. I didn't like Malcolm's affidavit. I believed the state of New York should have kept John Hill imprisoned for as long as it could for the death of my father or denied him parole for his original convictions.

Meeting the Attica Prosecutor

I made it known to FVOA members that I might not be onboard with the solicitation of help from Malcolm. Jonathan Gradess suggested that I talk to Malcolm myself, and, as I would learn, this would be typical of Jonathan. He was a great leader, and he, like Gary Horton, was providing us solid legal advice pro bono. Jonathan had a way of letting you—on your own—reach the answer he believed was the right one. He'd guide you to that answer instead of beating you over the head with his opinion. Or he would ask you uncomfortable and pointed questions until you had no defense left.

Instead of defending Malcolm Bell, Jonathan instead recommended that the two of us talk. Jonathan always insisted that I should see the riot from many different perspectives, and now I am glad that he did.

I didn't place the call immediately. Much like my hesitancy to speak with Frank, I waited several weeks. But this hesitancy was different. In Frank's case, I worried about how he would respond to me. With Malcolm, I was more concerned about how I might react to him and whether his actions on behalf of Hill would anger me these many years after he'd provided the affidavit on Hill's behalf.

I also told my mother that I might call Malcolm Bell, reminding her of his role in John Hill's release. She let me know that she wasn't pleased with the idea of us connecting or of his coming to the assistance of FVOA. I told her that I felt the same way.

Still, Jonathan persisted in his inimitable way, and I did call Malcolm in the summer of 2000 during the months when I began to reach out to many who had experienced the riot through a different prism. I explained to Malcolm why I was calling. He already knew that I was one of the more active members of FVOA, and he understood why I might be reluctant to seek his help.

I let him know early in the conversation that I was upset with what he'd done nearly a quarter century before, and I wanted him to explain it to me. My family felt as if we'd never received justice for the death of my father, and it seemed as if Malcolm Bell had abetted the release of the man who had killed my dad.

Malcolm told me in no uncertain terms that his affidavit had not been a favor for John Hill. Nor, he said, did he think that Hill had not killed my father. Instead, he had no reason to fault the jury's verdict, based on the evidence before it. But Malcolm believed the law was clear and it was inappropriate and illegal for Hill to be held any longer. The law, Malcolm said, must apply equally to all, even John Hill. Governor Carey had ensured that kidnapping and other charges against inmates were dropped—just as he also halted prosecutions of police—but Hill's murder conviction was left in place. Malcolm did not think Hill should be treated differently than other prisoners.

I knew in my heart that he was right, but nonetheless I didn't like the answer.

Malcolm said that his affidavit had been an act of protecting a citizen's rights. But I didn't care if John Hill's rights were protected. I didn't care if his rights were run over. I didn't care if he received extra prison time for the death of my father.

Malcolm was sympathetic. He said he recognized how difficult those times must have been for my family. "I'm sure this is terrible for you," he said. "But, out of a commitment to the law, I felt it was necessary for me to write this."

We talked at length about the affidavit, and my mind was not completely changed. But, as I would learn, when Malcolm talks, he can melt you. He is a soft-spoken man, and one whose integrity is knitted into every word he says and every fiber of his being. A Quaker, he seeks to do what is right and just, regardless of the cost to himself. He does not deviate from actions because of the sentiments of others who might be angered. That is why he became the Attica whistleblower; that is why he helped free the man convicted of murdering my father.

Meeting the Attica Prosecutor

I slowly came around to welcoming Malcolm as a voice for FVOA, but I knew that others in the group might be wary. Malcolm had sought to put some police in prison for their alleged crimes at Attica. The sympathies of many in our membership for law enforcement could make welcoming Malcolm Bell a hard sale.

Michael Smith was one of those who thought Malcolm could help FVOA. The two knew each other because Michael had been a witness before the grand jury when Malcolm was a prosecutor. As Malcolm would later say, Michael was the only witness he ever asked "to drop his drawers." Michael showed his wounds, the four entry wounds in his abdomen. The evidence appeared obvious that Michael had been shot with an automatic AR-15, meaning that Michael was likely shot by a fellow corrections officer. The state troopers were not carrying AR-15's. The arsenal at Attica held AR-15's used by corrections officers, and the records showed all the guns had been taken out of the prison arsenal on September 13.

Michael had long thought he was purposefully shot by a fellow corrections officer, though why would be a mystery. Perhaps Michael had been too chummy with the inmates. Plus, the interviews Michael gave the media while he was hostage were damning of the state. Maybe someone was offended by that.

Michael's wounds were so precise that he suspected he had been targeted. Malcolm also came to believe that Michael was not struck by stray gunfire, as initial investigations into the riot—including the McKay Commission probe—had determined.

Michael and others who thought Malcolm could be a powerful voice for FVOA recommended that we meet him in person. In September 2000, he and his wife Nancy drove from their Vermont home to Attica and joined us at QWL.

Malcolm acknowledged the animosity toward him, but that didn't deter him. He told us of his experiences and answered our questions with an assured ease. That is one of Malcolm's traits: He has a staggering confidence. It is not arrogance; instead, it is his desire for justice. And he displayed it that night at QWL. If someone questioned his push for prosecutions, he would respond with an understanding of why the question was being asked. And he would return to the law and the need that it be applied equitably for all if it is to mean anything. In the end, he tied up his presentation in a nice bow and had us on his side.

In 1985 Malcolm released a book entitled *The Turkey Shoot: Tracking the Attica Cover-Up*, which told the story of his history as the Attica prosecutor. The book was updated in 2017 and retitled as *The Attica Turkey Shoot: Carnage, Cover-Up, and the Pursuit of Justice*.

In the book, Malcolm writes of his meeting with FVOA and of his subsequent support for our organization.

"I found myself deeply moved to stand before this group of aging men and women and their adult children whose pain I had only read about," Malcolm wrote. "They had given up so much to serve the State; in return the State had treated them like jetsam."

Malcolm wrote about an emotional hug he received from Carl Valone's daughter, Maryann, while he also acknowledged that some of our members were slow to approach him: "Some of them seemed shy. Some were hard to read. I felt that it was only natural if some of them resented my past efforts to prosecute their fellow law officers, yet they were as deserving of recompense as all the others."

Any lingering bitterness I might have had toward Malcolm was gone by the time of his meeting with us. We had continued to talk before he came to the QWL, and I saw how committed he was to doing the right thing. He, too, had been led to believe that the state had taken care of us in the aftermath of the riot. He was as surprised as anyone to learn that the opposite was true. He was also surprised to learn how men and women who were neighbors and friends and relatives had gone so long without discussing our mistreatment among one another. But once he learned the truth, he offered to help in any way he could.

Writing more about FVOA in *The Attica Turkey Shoot*, Malcolm said of our lobbying and our demands: "Their quest, then, depended upon the decency of New York State officials—as we have seen, not a rosy prospect. But they clearly had enormous moral authority, and they sought to bring it to bear on then-Governor George Pataki, a Republican, and other officials in every way they could think of.

"The main mover of their campaign was a cheerful dynamo named Deanne Quinn Miller, the eldest of the three daughters of murdered Correction[s] Officer William Quinn."

By the time Malcolm wrote those words in 2015, he and I had become dear friends, as had our families. Malcolm has friends and family in western New York, and he and Nancy often add a visit to our Batavia home when they travel to the area. Nancy once told me that she and Malcolm considered me to be another daughter. I never could have envisioned a relationship like the one we now have, and there is no shortage of irony that Attica, as ugly as it was and as painful as it was for me, brought me in contact with people like Malcolm who are now so significant in my life.

After one trip to Albany, during which Gary and I had a meeting with Jonathan, we then drove to the Bells' home, less than two hours away. The day's activities had clearly left a mark on me, because I began screaming during the night, suffering from an Attica-related nightmare.

It was embarrassing; I woke up the entire house. I was sleeping in the spacious first floor living room, which had a large window to a wooded backyard. During the previous day, Malcolm had told us how bears would sometimes wander up to the window. Malcolm was sure the story of the bears had triggered my nightmare. He was so sweet after I'd calmed down. "I'm sorry," he said. "Maybe I shouldn't have mentioned the bears."

Were it not for Malcolm, I never would have met another figure central to the history of Attica—former *New York Times* reporter, editor, and columnist, Tom Wicker, who died in 2011.

Wicker had been one of the citizen observers at Attica. He was selected by the inmates because he had written sympathetically of George Jackson, an activist and inmate who was fatally shot during an attempted escape from San Quentin prison only weeks before Attica exploded.

He had also written the foreword to Malcolm's first edition of *The Turkey Shoot*, saying: "Malcolm Bell is an American hero, a brave man who risked his livelihood, his profession, and the good opinion of his peers for the sake of truth and justice."

Noting his own role in the riot, Wicker wrote that, "I don't expect ever to be entirely free of Attica—most particularly of the corrosive sense of terrible failure, a failure of men and procedures, of courage and wisdom, of compassion, or the true toughness of spirit that knows no fear. Still, Attica had its few heroes, and to that short but honorable list this book will add the name of Malcolm Bell."

Tom Wicker and his wife, Pamela—a former ABC and CNN producer—lived about an hour from Malcolm and Nancy in Rochester, Vermont. They had purchased a 160-acre farm, literally an entire side of a Vermont mountain.

Malcolm arranged for Gary and me to meet Wicker on a day after we'd made the Albany trip. Malcolm and Nancy remained friends with Wicker and his wife, Pamela.

Typically, the drive between the two Vermont homes would have been a leisurely hour. But a torrential storm had washed out bridges and flooded roads. I rode with Nancy, who was driving a Honda sports utility vehicle, and we followed Malcolm and Gary, who was driving his GMC Canyon.

Gary, following Malcolm's directions, led the way, and there were times when the road completely disappeared. Nancy drove the standard transmission SUV as if she were unbothered by the conditions or the occasional lack of roadway.

At one point, we were literally driving in a creek bed, with water splashing up onto the windshield and Nancy calmly flipping on the wipers for visibility. The drive was much longer than the usual hour that Malcolm said it was. We eventually reached the farm, the home sitting on a huge mound surrounded with water from the storm, much like a moat around a castle.

In the home, we were greeted with welcome and warmth. Tom Wicker was then very ill, but he was of a generation that required that he be well-attired and his hair neatly combed for our visit. Just as with Malcolm, or with Frank, nothing was off-limits in our conversation. And, just as with another observer, Arthur Eve, Tom Wicker was clearly haunted by his recollections of Attica. He, too, seemed to think that somehow he could have changed the outcome, that he could have done something different as a negotiator that would have altered the bloodshed that was to come.

Speaking about the day of the retaking, Wicker once told an interviewer that on that September 13 morning he lost his "lifelong belief... that the state was there to protect us.

"I lost my faith in the state, and I haven't had any since," he said, clarifying that he was speaking about our government as a whole. "I don't mean I'm unpatriotic at all. But [for] most people, it seems to me sometimes patriotism is taken to be faith."

At this moment in the filmed interview, Wicker punctuated his thoughts with both fists thrust into the air, physically emphasizing the word "faith" as if a declaration of exuberant patriotism.

Then his voice quieted, his hands dropped, and he somberly said, "I don't have that faith anymore."

The Prison Guard's Daughter

As I learned when meeting people like Wicker and Arthur Eve, the burdens they carried were indicative of their unwavering humanity. They should not have felt responsible for the deaths at Attica. Yet those responsible for the deaths—the inmates who killed my father, the officials who approved the violent retaking, the police who stormed the prison, the governor who refused to talk to the inmates and intervene in negotiations—seemed to believe they bore no responsibility. Nor would they accept any.

There were times in our conversation with Tom Wicker when he would stop, clearly fatigued. Once he regrouped, Malcolm would lead him back to just where the conversation had paused. Pamela had told us that his health was deteriorating and we should not expect other opportunities to talk to him. And she graciously allowed us to continue, as did Tom himself.

The talk was emotional for him, but he knew it meant so much to us and to him, as well, to have this conversation, no matter how painful. We talked for hours, before saying our goodbyes. We were driving back to western New York—an eight-hour drive home—and thankfully Tom provided a route that did not include submerged roads.

The meeting with Tom Wicker had enlivened me, despite the rough travel day we'd had. I didn't stop talking the entire ride home; replaying what Tom had said had given me a lot to think about. Poor Gary—I piled question after question on him, rehashing what Tom told us. But I was now seeing Attica as a large puzzle, and I kept finding new pieces to fit into the history I was learning.

As of this writing, Malcolm and Nancy no longer live in the home where we visited numerous times. In their late 80s, they have moved into an independent retirement community elsewhere in Vermont.

They now live on Tom Wicker Lane, a happy coincidence.

CHAPTER FOURTEEN

Taking Our Case Public

There was another reason Malcolm Bell quickly endeared himself to our group: Our members discovered that he, too, was a victim of Attica.

As a whistleblower who'd received media coverage nationwide, Malcolm found his world completely pulled out from beneath him. He could not find a job again in the corporate sector. His first marriage ended in divorce. The father of two young boys, he left the home and could not see them as frequently as he preferred. It was a painful schism for him. Our group, once it realized how much he'd lost and given up by choosing to do the right thing, became more welcoming and accepting of him.

We even asked him to join us at what would be our first major public presentation, a panel in late September 2000 at Genesee Community College in Batavia.

We in FVOA were learning from our lobbying and the occasional media interviews that our stories—most of which had been untold—had power. Most of the public assumed that we'd been well taken care of in the aftermath of Attica.

We also realized that we needed bigger forums, and Genesee Community College (GCC) offered us one. The administration there knew about our organization and wanted to have a panel discussion about Attica. Gary Horton helped make it happen. As he told the media the days before the event, our aim was twofold: To let the world know how we were treated and to also let the world know the identity and mission of FVOA.

We did not know what to expect or how many would attend the session at the college's fine arts theater. It ended up packed, with over three hundred people.

We opened the session with one of the videos of the retaking. For those who have never seen the videos, the chaos is palpable. The cacophony of gunfire is relentless; at least 2,200 bullets, shotgun pellets, and shells were fired in the retaking and, in addition to the thirty-nine slain, another eighty-nine people were injured. The tear gas is so thick that anyone who sees the video cannot help but wonder how police expected to lay siege to the prison without killing hostages.

That video set the stage for what was to come with our stories. Gary's wife, Debbie, who also helped arrange the panel, told the silent crowd, "Pain does not have an expiration date. There is no statute of limitations on pain."

Michael Smith was on the panel, as were G.B. Smith, Malcolm Bell and me. William Cunningham, the lawyer for Lynda Jones, joined us and told how he still had the check that the Attica widow had wisely refused to cash. Cunningham had said he would be there to help us whenever needed. He served as a reminder that the one widow who did not accept state financial "assistance" was the only one who had received any meaningful restitution.

"I feel so bad for the [surviving] hostages," Cunningham told the GCC crowd. "You're here like you're begging the state of New York for something. They owe you. They owe you."

Joining Michael were other hostage survivors. Each told their story, with Michael again recalling that the inmates had given him an earlier version of their manifesto and how it sought little more than basic humanitarian treatment. G. B. Smith told of the original eruption of the riot and how he was assaulted and dragged into the D Yard as a hostage.

"They took my nightstick and beat my rear end with it," he said in what was his inimitable way of telling of his experiences.

This event marked the first time we'd spoken to a crowd of any size, and it was draining on all of us. But you could truly hear a pin drop throughout our presentations. We took questions from the audience, and we began to develop a rhythm that night. If I struggled to answer a question, Michael or Malcolm or Gary would sense my difficulties and step in. As the years passed, and we added more presentations—some to large crowds, some to small classrooms—Michael and I would joke that we could tell of each other's experiences word for word if asked to do so. I could even replicate Michael's pregnant pauses.

After the panel, we could not leave for another hour or two because of the number of people who approached with more questions or wanted to tell of their own connections to the riot, even if those connections were tenuous.

I met a woman who had been a maid at one of the nearby hotels in Batavia that housed the State Police who were stationed outside the prison for the days of negotiations and during and after the retaking. When one shift left, she immediately cleaned the rooms because she knew another shift would be arriving soon thereafter for rest.

There were people who had relatives with some connection to the riot, or we'd hear from individuals who simply remembered having a state trooper blowing by them at ninety miles per hour the day the riot broke out, with the troopers en route to the prison. In western New York, the Attica riot was almost like the Kennedy assassination, in that everyone seemed to recall just where they were when they heard of the uprising.

Our presentations, including the one at GCC and others we would do in weeks to months to come, proved to the state that we were here to stay. We wanted to shame the state into dealing with us and our demands. And the panels served as a barometer, telling us that we would get people to hear us and the media to cover us.

Malcolm had also enlisted Tom Wicker for help, and he brought even greater statewide and national recognition to FVOA. The same week as the GCC forum, Wicker published an opinion column in the *New York Times* about our plight.

"So far, New York has done nothing remotely adequate to compensate these forgotten victims for what one investigatory commission called 'the bloodiest encounter between Americans since the Civil War,'" Wicker wrote. "In some cases, the state has deceived widows and survivors. And no state administration, Republican or Democratic, has admitted responsibility for the uprising at the overcrowded prison, for its poorly planned and brutal repression or for the forty-three resulting deaths."

Throughout 2000 and into 2001 our lobbying continued. Jonathan, we learned, was known by almost everyone in Albany who mattered. And many people seemed to fear Jonathan. He had traveled in the Albany power circles for years, fighting successfully for indigent clients, and he knew just how to craft an argument that would either convince or embarrass lawmakers into doing what was right (or doing what Jonathan wanted them to do). Jonathan was able to voice what seemed like a threat, yet in a veiled way that made people unsure just how far he would go.

We saw this early in our negotiations. We were still talking to Senator Dale Volker, but Jonathan had also succeeded in getting us an audience with the counsel for Governor George Pataki. That was a major victory. State officials told us that we were embarrassing the corrections department with stories about our mistreatment. Jonathan let it be known that far worse embarrassment would come if we were not listened to.

Jonathan often referred to the South African Truth and Reconciliation Commission, which he thought could serve as a template for how the state should respond to FVOA. Established by the South African government, the commission publicly aired the horrors of apartheid. Prompted by Jonathan, I would read some of the records of the commission, including the transcripts of those who testified before it. I could not read all of them; some were simply too painful.

Connecting with the governor's legal counsel was also helpful because it helped us take our issues to someone with significant power other than Senator Volker. Volker had been a policeman in the small Erie County village of Depew at the time of the riot, and he told us that he had responded to the uprising. We were never clear about just what he did, if anything, at Attica, because the Depew police department surely had no role in the retaking. But Volker would often speak of the riot as if he had some secretive inside knowledge that those of us who lived it, including even the hostages, did not. He was usually unwilling to accept that the state erred in any way at Attica, and he constantly defended the decisions made in September 1971. The relationship grew incredibly strained. The irony was that he was a "law and order" public official, one whose politics should have endeared him to many of our members, but instead members of FVOA grew to resent him.

In one conversation, Volker said he had difficulty collaborating with us because Malcolm Bell was now in our ranks. He claimed that the State Police originally surged into D Yard because of the claims that Frank Smith had killed a hostage, a statement not supported by any history of the riot. He told me that my father was a hero, just as were the State Police who retook the prison, even if thirty-nine people died.

Volker would often say that we were being guided by "misinformation," and he would spout some claims about what happened at Attica that were wholly unsupported.

The Prison Guard's Daughter

We continued to try to work with Volker and Arthur Eve, the lawmaker who was far more receptive to our group and who had experienced Attica in ways that he could never shake. And as I was finding my voice while telling my story to panels and interviewers, I discovered that I could go head-to-head with those in positions of power who wanted us to disappear. I saw how Jonathan could successfully badger them, and I knew that I could have equal success because no one could question just what I'd lost in September 1971.

We had our list of demands, and we would not budge from it. We were negotiable with the restitution. We recognized that $50 million could be more than we would ever see, but we also knew that the $550,000 the state had tried to give us was not enough.

Working with Jonathan and Gary, I became one of our most active and persistent lobbyists, the "dynamo" that Malcolm would later call me in his book. And I knew we were making headway, even if we encountered resistance. That resistance just made me more relentless.

In March 2001, it became obvious that state officials knew they had to reckon with us. That month, Governor George Pataki decided to create a task force that would hear our concerns and try to resolve them. Pataki's panel was to be headed by Glenn Goord, the top official in the state corrections department. The state Legislature's leading Republican would appoint a member, as would the top legislative Democrat.

Arthur Eve, thankfully, was the Democratic choice. Volker was the Republican.

While I may not have been totally pleased with the task force composition, we were now on the state government radar in a way we had never been before. Looking back, I now appreciate how hard we worked.

We were just over a year beyond the live radio show at the Signature Café in Attica, and the governor of New York now recognized us.

George Pataki realized we were not going away.

CHAPTER FIFTEEN

Meeting Richard

During that same summer of 2000, we learned that New York City filmmaker Brad Lichtenstein was making a documentary about the plight of the Attica inmates. It wasn't the sort of film likely to appeal to our members, many of whom had been approached by film people over the years. We were, in general, distrusting and leery.

Then Brad decided he wanted to talk to us.

A former producer for PBS's Bill Moyers, Brad had learned of the formation of the Forgotten Victims of Attica through media coverage. He saw that we, too, were victims and were beginning to build momentum throughout the state. But, just as with Malcolm Bell, we were unsure if we could trust him.

Brad first contacted Gary Horton, and Gary was very protective of our group. Gary hit Brad with a barrage of questions: What were his intentions in interviewing our members? Was there a theme to his movie? How much did he really know about Attica?

Again, as with Malcolm, there is a gentle warmth with Brad, and Gary convinced me to talk to him. I was unsure, though for different reasons than I had been wary of Malcom at first.

The Prison Guard's Daughter

By the summer of 2000, Brad had spent months with Elizabeth Fink, Frank Smith, and other inmates in New York City, interviewing and filming them as they prepared for their testimony before Judge Telesca. And Brad came from a very different world than did our members. Could he truly understand us and what we'd been through?

Brad, however, had a truly humanitarian heart. Once he'd been part of a video team which worked for the rights of the homeless and was arrested filming Amtrak security police beating a homeless man. He later successfully sued the police—the case was settled—and he and others on the team gave the entirety of their award to programs for the homeless.

I finally agreed to talk to Brad, and during a visit to Rochester he came to Batavia to meet me. I remember being very guarded with him. After all, he'd spent a significant amount of time reviewing Liz Fink's records and speaking directly with inmates who had survived the riot. What would he know or understand about "our side?" I decided to take a chance and began to tell him my story of Attica and its effect on my life.

Brad told me how my story resonated with him because he had heard similar stories from the families of slain inmates.

"Did you ever think about the inmate families?" he asked me.

For much of my life, "inmates" fell under one category: Hill and Pernasilice, Murder and Assault. I really didn't know all the others, and from my perspective, they had little importance to me and my family.

Speaking with Brad further deepened my understanding that seeing the riot from only one perspective limited my ability to learn. Somehow these individuals were coming into my life—Jonathan, Frank, Malcolm, Brad—who saw the riot in a different context, and I was shedding the preconceptions and prejudices I'd held onto for years. It wasn't that I completely absolved the inmates for the riot, or especially for the death of my father, but the fact was there were good people in the prison population who'd suffered just as I had.

Meeting Richard

It was during a conversation with Brad that he told me about one of those prisoners—Richard X. Clark.

A Muslim activist (some would consider him radical), Clark had ended up in prison because of drugs. He'd begun using heavily while enlisted in the navy. After his 1968 discharge, his addictions—cocaine, heroin—pushed him to criminal activity.

He was arrested in 1969 for armed robbery. He then had a wife and one-year-old twin sons. A Bronx resident, Clark had also just passed the exam for the New York City Police Department.

It was in prison that Clark found the Muslim faith. He had been behind bars at several New York facilities before a transfer to Attica, and there he witnessed the appalling conditions. He drifted toward the Muslim worshippers and then joined their ranks. Charismatic and intelligent, he became a prison minister.

Unfortunately, the prison administration had little use for its Muslim inmates. Protestants, Catholics, and Jews all could worship at Attica, but there was no room, it seemed, for the Muslim congregation. They would gather in the prison yard, sometimes quietly, for meetings. Though there were dozens of Muslims at Attica, Clark could only bring six together at a time.

And while Clark and other Muslims had successfully sued the prison for pork-free meals, even if only for peanut butter and jelly sandwiches, the prison administration ignored the ruling.

The Attica administration also blocked books and magazines that Clark had ordered. Some focused on the Muslim religion and some on racism.

Once, as Clark would later explain, he'd complained to Prison Superintendent Vincent Mancusi about why he was not getting books that he knew had been shipped to him. Mancusi said he couldn't allow "that kind of material" to reach inmates.

"What kind of material?" Clark asked.

"It's those Black books," Mancusi answered. "That's the whole problem now."

When the riot broke out, Clark had been denied almost four months of mail that had been piled up in the mailroom. Like Frank, Clark became central to the security of the hostages. He brought together other Muslim inmates, and they created the protective circle for the captive prison employees. He also took on the role of negotiator. He was one of the men chosen in a democratic vote by inmates to be a leader in the Yard.

But Brad's main purpose in telling me about Richard Clark was to let me know that Richard had tried to save my father's life.

Royal Morgan had told me first-hand about his attempt to help my father after he found him beaten and unconscious, but I had no clear answers as to how my father finally was taken from the Times Square area and out of the prison. As Brad told me, Richard Clark had also seen my father, his skull fractured and his face bloodied. Clark gathered up several inmates—this was after Morgan had unsuccessfully tried to move my father—and they found a mattress in A block and placed my father on it.

There was much more to the story, Brad said, but he thought it best if I heard it directly from Richard Clark himself.

Brad had gotten to know Clark through his making of the film. I was unsure I wanted to take this step, and I spoke with my family. No one in my family, nor among former coworkers I'd asked, seemed to have a sense of just how my father was finally taken from the prison.

Gary, Michael, and I were planning a trip to New York City for some other FVOA business, so I weighed whether I wanted to set aside time to meet with Richard Clark while there.

I again talked to Brad.

"If you'd like to meet him, he'd like to meet you," Brad told me. That shook me more, the fact that he *wanted* to meet with me.

Meeting Richard

I didn't know Richard Clark at all, but I saw no reason for him to fabricate a story like this. After days of struggling to decide what to do, I finally told Brad I would see Clark.

Some weeks later, Gary, Michael, and I were in a Harlem restaurant, sitting across a table from Clark and others who also, as I was told, helped get my father to a prison gate so he could be safely removed. I hadn't slept for nights before, and my usual stomach problems, along with a migraine, had set in.

Clark had chosen the restaurant, above which was a Muslim school. Brad also had his team filming our meeting, which added another layer of anxiety. I did not want to misspeak, and I especially did not want to misspeak with the cameras rolling.

There were others eating in the restaurant, and I, along with my FVOA colleagues and Brad's team, were the only white people there. My Attica journey was taking me places I never imagined; this was surely one of them.

There is a gentleness with Richard Clark, not only when he speaks—as I also would discover that morning—but also in his appearance and how he carries himself. Bespectacled and bald, Richard still seemed to have the self-assurance he'd demonstrated in the Yard decades before as a spry and more militant version of the man I was meeting. There, in the hours after the initial burst, he had tried to bring some semblance of sanity to D Yard. He had organized a medical area; convinced inmates who were planning to use drugs that had earlier been smuggled in to them to turn in the illicit substances and hypodermic needles; and established the security detail.

I knew all of this about him from the books and histories I had read. Those books and histories did not tell me that Richard Clark had tried to save my dad.

As we sat there, with my nervousness quite evident, Clark wasted no time telling me what happened the morning of September 9, 1971.

In the initial flood of the chaos, Richard was making his way to the prison yard when he came upon Royal Morgan trying to lift and move my father. Morgan, as Clark recalled, pleaded with him for help. Clark rounded up other inmates and asked them to find a mattress.

Clark put Morgan in a cell with another officer whom they'd placed in there for his safety, and first went to the gate of A Block and found an officer. He urged him to get a doctor, but he was ignored.

When Clark got back to my father, he was now on the mattress, unconscious. Other prisoners were there, and they lifted the mattress— my father still on it—and carried it down a flight of stairs.

One of the other men at the restaurant was more vocal and animated than the soft-spoken yet confident Clark. This man, Brother Shariff as he was called, had also helped carry my father.

He pointed to a chipped tooth in his mouth and told me he'd lost a portion of his tooth trying to help my father. As they carried the mattress down a hallway, the floor was soaked with blood and water, he said. He lost his footing and began to fall. He wanted to keep my father on the mattress because of the severity of his injuries.

"I didn't want to drop your dad," he told me. "I didn't want him to hit the floor because of his head injuries."

He managed to keep my father balanced on the mattress while taking the brunt of a fall with his face.

"I broke this tooth in half carrying your dad," he said, again showing me the tooth that was only partially there.

The inmates got the mattress and my father to a gate at the prison administration building. There, they told officers on the other side of the gate, as well as Prison Superintendent Vincent Mancusi, that my father was in dire need of medical help. No one responded, either fearful to come back into the prison or, perhaps, simply uncaring.

I would later piece together some of just what happened to my father afterward and learn that he may have lay there on the mattress for well over an hour. I was able to get hospital information about when he arrived there on September 9, injured. And, as I discovered, some officers who checked into the prison at the initial outbreak of the riot, hoping to gain control of some of the inmate blocks, said they saw my father on the mattress as they clocked in. They had been regimented to know that if they failed to punch in with the time clock, then they wouldn't get paid.

It seemed so contrary to the brotherhood of officers, the belief—like soldiers in combat—that you leave no one behind.

At the end of our conversation, I asked Richard Clark if I could contact him if I had more questions, and he assured me he would welcome that.

And we did talk occasionally, but sadly, he again returned to drugs.

One Christmas season I telephoned him, and a woman answered the cellphone number I then had for him. He was then at a drug treatment center and could not take phone calls. I tried to explain to the woman our strange connection—Richard had been at Attica, he'd helped my father, we talked sometimes.

"Richard carried my father on a mattress," I said. "It would mean a lot if I could talk to him."

I think she thought I was either insane or persistent or so insanely persistent that she figured she had no choice but to get Richard.

Richard came to the telephone, and I could tell the conversation was difficult for him. He said he hoped this would be his last time in treatment as a resident—he had worked as a counselor—and he wanted to leave treatment clean for good.

I told him I was praying that he would have the strength to get through, and I was sure he would.

That was the last time we spoke. Richard Clark died the next year.

CHAPTER SIXTEEN

The Workmen's Compensation Ruse

We had another stop in New York City after visiting Richard Clark in November 2000—the Long Island home of Morris Jacobs.

Jacobs was retired after fifty years with a little-known state agency—the State Insurance Fund. He had read and heard about the Forgotten Victims of Attica and the treatment of widows and families in 1971, and promised he had information we would want to hear. He said he had proof that the state had purposefully deceived widows after the riot.

I was still struggling after meeting with Richard. My stomach was tossing wildly and my migraine pounding. When we walked into the home of Morris Jacobs—a round-faced man who stood slightly over five feet tall but was bursting with oversized energy—my condition had not improved much. His wife saw immediately that I was not well and asked what she could do. I asked if I could have some water or ginger ale, maybe some Motrin if available, and rest on a chair or couch. As Michael and Gary met with Jacobs, I laid down on a family sofa. Later, though the weather was wintry and wet, I returned to our rental car and slept in the backseat. I was completely overwhelmed, emotionally and physically.

The Workmen's Compensation Ruse

Jacobs's half century with the State Insurance Fund (SIF) and his rise from the bowels of the agency to a major leadership role made him a walking encyclopedia on the institution. Even the history that preceded him, he knew in great detail: how the catastrophic Triangle Shirtwaist factory fire in lower Manhattan in 1911 had revealed the lack of worker protections; how workers' compensation protections were enshrined in state laws after the blaze, which killed 146 people, many of them teenage women; and how the role of the State Insurance Fund grew significantly in the decades after its origin.

Jacobs joined the agency in 1943, the same year he was drafted into military service. He would receive a Purple Heart and two Bronze Stars in World War II before returning to the SIF as a low-level clerk. As the years passed, he constantly took promotion exams and kept ascending into new jobs. In the 1980s he became the director of claims, one of the top positions at the SIF, and stayed in the job for around a decade until his 1995 retirement.

But it was 1971 that Jacobs wanted to talk about. That year he had the title of Associate Compensation Claims Examiner, a midlevel supervisor. The Attica riot, he said, was one of the most horrendous episodes in terms of loss confronted by the state's insurance program. It was expected there would be a slew of lawsuits against New York from prison employees and their families.

Jacobs was not then in a position directly involved with possible litigation from the riot, but he recalled meeting with a high-ranking SIF official who was. Jacobs asked about the possibility of significant claims against the state and the likely major payout, and, as he recalled, he received a very cryptic answer.

"We'll be taking care of it," he was told. Jacobs didn't know just what that answer meant, and he didn't follow up.

Years later, when he heard of FVOA, Jacobs realized that the widows had been cheated by the state.

He heard how the widows had been approached in the days after the deaths and promised that they would continue to receive checks. This in itself was abnormal, Jacobs said. The SIF had a policy that no contact can be made to the next of kin without an appearance before a compensation judge. It was the judge's job to advise the person so that they could choose the workers' compensation payment or not. If not, they could sue.

In our case, the state would typically wait two months or more to ensure a widow had proper legal representation. Insurance carriers also preferred this, Jacobs said, so there were not entanglements later, such as cases in which payments were actually made to the wrong individuals. The State Insurance Fund had an inflexible rule, he said: Widows or widowers were not approached if you knew they weren't represented by an attorney or had not clearly declined legal representation.[1]

Obviously, from what Jacobs said, the state had set out to save itself millions by taking advantage of the vulnerability and suffering of the Attica widows and employees. If the agency wanted to offer condolences, that would've been fine. But SIF employees should never have offered workers' compensation payments.

Here was the most maddening thing, which we in FVOA knew and Jacobs did not: The state workers had not even mentioned the workers' compensation payments to most of the widows and the employees who were encouraged to take time off after surviving the riot. Instead, workers' compensation payments were slipped into the checks without even a mention of where the money came from. The checks the widows and workers received looked just like their normal paychecks.

To this day, I believe this to be the most insidious thing the state did after Attica. These were just regular people, loyal and committed state

---

1   While writing this book, we discovered that there was at least one other exception to the SIF's inflexible rule.

workers, who were doing their job, and they wound up cheated by their employers.

I've often wondered whether my mother would have turned down the payment from the state if she'd known what it might cost her. She had unknowingly chosen the workers' compensation as the "election of remedy," and, unlike Lynda Jones, she could not sue.

But I know she was struggling to survive, simply trying to put food on the table and a roof over our heads. Any money then was welcome, but I don't know if she, or many of the other widows for that matter, would have known to get legal help. By SIF policy, they should have been given the chance, and they were purposely not.

Years later, when we discussed this at a FVOA meeting, the widows were furious. They felt they'd been taken advantage of in a disgusting way. That anger helped galvanize and unite them, including when it came to declining the state's restitution offer of $550,000.

Morris Jacobs had evidence that we did not—the state had acted maliciously to save itself millions in 1971. And he had no hesitancy letting it be known. The widows had received worse treatment than the criminally accused, who are at least read their Miranda rights, he said.

"Did anybody read the rights of these widows during this vulnerable position, just a few days after the fatality? And then within two weeks they get a first payment of compensation which precluded them from suing the state," Jacobs would later say.

Jacobs was righteously and justifiably mad, and he said he'd help however he could. Michael and Gary agreed to return at a later date and take a deposition from him to be added to our lobby's ammunition. Morris Jacobs was telling us what we always thought to be true, and we intended to use his allegations to show the world how the state had turned its back on the Attica widows. Or, even more infuriating, how the state had intentionally manipulated them.

Gary and Michael were excited about what we'd learned from Morris Jacobs after we left his home and drove back to John F. Kennedy International Airport for our flight to Rochester. I couldn't share in the excitement then. I still felt like hell. I thought my head would explode as I lay in the backseat of the car on the drive to the airport.

The flight back was not much better. I was squeezed into a middle seat between Gary, who was watching the Cooking Channel, and Michael, who was watching cartoons. I was trying to stay focused on home improvement shows on HGTV, but, moments before landing, I started feeling violently ill.

Just as the flight attendants were alerting us to buckle our belts, put our seats in the upright position, and raise our trays, I knew I was going to be sick, very sick. I almost leap-frogged over Gary's lap to get to the lavatory. A flight attendant tried to intervene, telling me I had to return to my seat. I'm sick, I said. No exceptions, she told me.

Too damn bad, I thought, and rushed into the lavatory. There I was, throwing up in an airplane lavatory, just as the plane made what thankfully was a smooth landing.

I left the bathroom under the glare of the flight attendant. Lady, I thought, if you knew the day I've had, you'd be offering me a drink right now.

CHAPTER SEVENTEEN

Task Force Heats Up

The negotiations with the Governor Pataki-appointed task force started out rocky. There were disagreements over restitution amounts, whether the state should fund counseling, whether the records could be opened, since many were sealed by court order, and whether one state administration could apologize for the actions of another.

The task force at first only showed a willingness for the Forgotten Victims of Attica to hold the annual ceremony at the prison. And, in truth, it wasn't the task force itself that seemed unbending; it was Corrections Commissioner Glenn Goord, whom the governor had chosen to lead the task force.

I had been skeptical about the task force from the outset, knowing that Senator Volker and Commissioner Goord were members. After all, our history with both of them had not been positive. Volker continued to treat his assistance with FVOA as more of a grand favor than as his legislative responsibility. And with Goord I felt we would relive the same treatment we'd come to expect from the state of New York. So here we were again, with the state investigating the state. Honestly, I had little faith in the process, and it may have reflected in my attitude. It was like the McKay Commission, whose work had left false impressions about what had happened at Attica—impressions since rebutted by history.

Still, I held out some hope. I needed to.

Then, we strongly suggested to the task force that we wanted our stories to be made into a historical record.

Our group did not see this as a problematic request. As group members traveling the state telling our stories, it was evident how little was known about us, our fight and our history, even within our surrounding communities. Not only did we want to rectify this but we also wanted to be sure there would be a lasting record.

We wrote a letter to the task force members, proposing public hearings—anyone who wanted to attend could come and listen—and we wanted testimony from our members. Jonathan Gradess again invoked the South African Truth and Reconciliation Commission with our group and emphasized how the commission had been cathartic for those who testified. That preserved testimony also ensured that the world would forever know of the horrors of apartheid.

The task force—again, Goord in particular—pushed back. My guess is that Arthur Eve was supportive of something like the hearings we proposed, but Goord was running the show.

It became obvious to us that the state again wanted little history of our treatment, nothing archived where, God forbid, people would have the ability to read it for generations to come.

We continued to make little headway with our back-and-forth correspondence, so we scheduled a meeting at the QWL in Attica. The task force insisted that no one other than those who would negotiate for our group could be present, even though many FVOA members wanted to attend this meeting, if just to observe. It was a minor hurdle, and we didn't argue much over it.

As it turned out, we had plenty else to argue over.

Task Force Heats Up

The task force members came, along with corrections department counselor Anthony Annucci, who would later take over the corrections department leadership and support us far more than his predecessors.

Gary and Jonathan represented us, along with some members, including Michael and me. Glenn Goord made sure at the beginning of the meeting that we knew he was in charge, armed with detailed plans for how the discussion would progress. At one point after we first sat down, Gary started to comment, and Goord told him, "You'll have your time."

Having two public defenders leading the negotiations for us turned out to be a blessing. They're accustomed to being knocked by those who don't see the value of representation for the indigent. They're accustomed to dealing with far fewer resources in criminal cases than the prosecution and police. And they are unyielding in their push for justice, regardless of how much opposition they face.

Jonathan was fluent in "Albany-speak," knowing how to bargain within governmental circles. And he could be withering with his sarcastic comebacks during tough negotiations. It became clear at the QWL that the state did not want open testimony meetings. They favored limited testimony from FVOA group members and other "witnesses," and they did not plan or want a court reporter for transcripts. I can still hear Jonathan responding, "So we all believe that these stories are very important, but you would not like us to invite all of the family members, supporting witnesses, nor would you like this to be public, and you don't want this to be recorded."

Jonathan spoke so pointedly that you could almost feel the dart go through your body if you were on the other side of his barbs.

The meeting was confrontational, so much so that at one point we agreed to take a break and we went to different locations outdoors on the QWL property. I was really upset at the tone that was being used during the meeting. It seemed dismissive and condescending, as if they knew what was best for us. I had worked my way around Albany enough to know they were trying to manipulate the outcome, do what was best for the state, while convincing us it was best for us too. I was not used to discussions so adversarial, however, and I was a little rattled during our break.

I had similar feelings in later talks with task force members and state legislators—a sense that we were coming "hat in hand" with our requests for help. That was always the rub for me. I knew I was in a righteous position, but I was often made to feel otherwise. I knew the FVOA mission was to have the state understand the degree of our loss, the tragedy, sadness, even depression that existed in our group. There was *plenty* of tragedy to go around in the aftermath of the riot. Yet I still felt as if I were pleading for our pain to be recognized and acknowledged.

During the short break, Gary and Jonathan were at ease, clearly in their element more than the rest of us. They calmed us. Gary would later tell me how much he and Jonathan enjoyed the hard bargaining and intensity of the meeting. They were on their turf, while I wasn't on mine.

We went back in, averse to the state demands for limited and private testimony. We were having none of that. The hearings would be public, and any FVOA members—surviving hostages, employees at the prison in September 1971, relatives of the slain—would be allowed to testify.

And there would be a court reporter transcribing the proceedings. We wanted the record available online, so that anyone—especially our relatives—could find it with ease and at any time.

We would not budge, and, eventually, that became clear to all. The task force began to accept our demands, while still hesitant to agree to one of our requests—a proposal to have "expert witnesses" at the hearings.

We had a list of witnesses we wanted, individuals like Malcolm Bell, with his background into the state intrusion into his investigation, and Morris Jacobs, who would tell how the state had handled the widows.

We also wanted Dr. George Abbott, who had been an assistant medical examiner in Monroe County and who helped perform the autopsies on those killed at Attica. He could tell how all those killed during the retaking were killed by police gunfire and not by inmates. That reality had long been known, but there were still some people, including the relatives of some in our group, who wanted to believe the inmates were the killers.

We planned to have lawyer William Cunningham testify; he was counsel for Lynda Jones and could speak to how much money she received. Attorney Eugene Tenney, who had tried to see if some of the hostages could sue the state, was also on our proposed witness list.

After resistance, the task force agreed to those witnesses. There were others we wanted, whom the task force nixed, and we agreed to forego. One was a National Guard medic who'd been in the Yard at Attica after the retaking. He had also been in Vietnam, and he'd told us how the bloodshed and wounds he'd witnessed at Attica were worse than what he'd confronted during the war. He wanted to help us however he could, but we agreed that he, and some others, would not testify.

We knew that the testimony could not be crammed into a day. Far more time would be needed.

We agreed to set up three separate sessions, each with two days of testimony. Four of the days would be held at the Rochester Institute of Technology University (RIT), with two in Albany, where we were likely to get more legislative and media attention.

Within my family, I explained how historical these hearings could be, and we decided we all should testify—myself, my mom, and my sisters, Christine and Amy. We decided that we did not want to be redundant, so we planned our testimony in earnest, with each of us focusing on how the murder of my father impacted us individually.

My mother was unsure at first but became convinced how important her testimony would be. When she also heard other widows planned to testify, she felt more comfortable with the idea.

Plus, she loved my father so dearly, and this would give her a chance to tell of that love and how special he was to her.

The hearings would be held in the spring and summer of 2002, more than thirty years after my father was murdered. My mother had said so little about my father for years, but now she was ready and willing to do just that.

Now we were making sure that the survivors of Attica would not be forgotten. Nor would Bill Quinn.

CHAPTER EIGHTEEN

The Pains of 9/11

The Forgotten Victims of Attica was gaining momentum. The governor's task force had been formed, and we'd developed continued communications with counsel to the governor.

The year 2001, we realized, gave us an opportunity to do much more. This would be the thirtieth anniversary of the riot, and there was likely to be no shortage of media coverage. Brad Lichtenstein's film, *The Ghosts of Attica*, was scheduled for release on Court TV only days before the riot anniversary, and we, after our initial wariness, had done multiple interviews for the film.

Throughout 2001, we mapped out plans for a five-day vigil at the Attica park and a march from the park to the prison, about half a mile. Our support from corrections unions across the country was growing, and officers from the East Coast to the West agreed to attend the vigil and the march, even though many had to pay for their own travel and use their own personal time.

Our media reach had grown far more expansive. The *New York Times* wrote about our vigil plans, and the left-leaning *Village Voice* interviewed members, including me, for an article on the approaching thirtieth anniversary.

In the *Village Voice* article, I explained the breadth of perspectives within FVOA. As I told reporter Jennifer Gonnerman, there were some members who believed the state troopers acted properly in the retaking and "they didn't want to kill anybody." There were others who thought the troopers had no concern for who was harmed or killed in the siege.

"I have family members who still think the guards were killed because the inmates slit their throats," I said. "But, you know, we're respectful of everybody's opinion."

"What does your organization want?" Gonnerman asked me.

"One of the things that our group wants more than any kind of money is [to be] acknowledged for who we are—people who got totally screwed out of this deal—and for the truth to be told," I said.

The approaching thirtieth anniversary presented us the chance to get that message out, a message that we hoped would exert additional pressure on the state task force. We were pleased with the task force's creation, but we did not intend to fall into silence. Public support would be our friend.

Our plans for the anniversary were far larger than anything we'd undertaken before. We would set up a tent at a park in Attica, and members would be there each of the five days—September 9 through September 13—with information about the uprising, FVOA, and our five demands and why they were important to us.

The vigil started on Sunday, September 9, 2001—only minutes after 9 a.m. Our choice of time for the start was purposeful, corresponding with the first sirens from the prison during the outbreak of the riot three decades before.

My sisters and I agreed to be at the table later on the day for September 11, 2001, as a remembrance of the anniversary of the death of our father. That was the morning when we heard the news: An American

Airlines 767 had crashed into the North Tower of the World Trade Center.

Like the rest of the world, we were stunned and unsure whether this was an awful accident or something else. Then news came of the second plane striking the Twin Towers and the subsequent terrorist attacks with other hijacked jetliners. September 11 had always been a day of grief for us, and it had now become one of suffering for an entire nation.

That morning, we were uncertain at first just what to do—not just with our presence at the Attica park but also with the days ahead. Several FVOA group members met to decide if we should cancel our plans, but we already had corrections officers in town, staying at nearby hotels. They had come from twelve states to support us, and we felt it imperative to push forward with the vigil just as planned.

As we grieved with our entire nation, we also still grieved for our father. We had come so far as an organization, and, while we knew that the days ahead would be difficult, we felt we could not abandon our cause at that time. Later that day, my sisters and I went to the Attica park tent as we'd planned.

It was a difficult decision for us, choosing to forge on at the same time as rescue workers were searching for survivors in the tons of rubble of the fallen Twin Towers. But we were certain we could do so respectfully, and our vigil continued.

The morning of September 13 came, and four hundred people gathered at the Attica park—corrections officers, Attica survivors and the families of those lost in the riot, and supporters from the community and beyond. The size of the crowd was proof that we'd made the right choice.

Malcolm Bell had also traveled to support us, as had Lynda Jones's attorney, William Cunningham, who'd driven from Florida because flights were grounded. They joined a group of speakers at the park, including Jonathan and corrections union representatives. Afterward, we all gathered for a half-mile-long march to the front of the prison for a somber memorial service. Leading the procession were two grandchildren of John Monteleone—eleven-year-old Ashley Herman and nine-year-old Robert Hyland. Carrying a Forgotten Victims of Attica banner, they were evidence of the multigenerational impact of the riot. Near the front, my husband, David, pushed our daughter, Cassidy, in a stroller, with Aubrey and me at his side.

We also acknowledged 9/11—as it would from then on be known—throughout the day. Speaking to the Rochester *Democrat and Chronicle*, my mother said that she and all of those in our ranks were thinking of the lives lost in New York City, Pennsylvania, and Washington, DC. Her words to the grieving families were those of someone who knew firsthand the heartache of loss.

"My heart goes out to all of those people," she said. "It will be a long road for them."

From that year on, September 11 would strike me even harder than it had in the many years prior when I would remember my father. There is an odd and painful symmetry in the two cataclysmic tragedies. Attica still stands as our nation's deadliest prison riot, and 9/11 as the worst terrorist attack upon our shores. No September 11 can pass for me without memories of both.

I was not alone among FVOA members. Later, at a FVOA hearing, Paula Krotz, whose husband was surviving hostage Paul Krotz, said, "Millions of Americans have Pearl Harbor and September 11, 2001, engraved on their psyche. We have Pearl Harbor, September 11, and Attica engraved on ours. Each has been horrific.

"However, Pearl Harbor was accomplished by the Japanese, September 11 was accomplished by the terrorists. But Attica was done to us by our own and we have lived with that illness since 1971."

And, as some of our members recognized in the days and months ahead, the state of New York reacted to 9/11 with the utmost sympathy for the families of the lost. Governor George Pataki suspended regulations that required workers' compensation claims to be made within thirty days. With us, workers' compensation was used to ensure we did not sue. The payments were duplicitously delivered to the grieving only days after the retaking in a way that appeared to be regular pay from the state.

If there was a positive to be found in our September 2001 vigil and memorial, it was this: We had support unlike any we could have imagined before. We had uniformed corrections officers from our own New York State Correctional Officers & Police Benevolent Association (NYSCOPBA), California Correctional Peace Officers Association (CCPOA), California Peace Officers Foundation (CPOF), Corrections USA (CUSA), and contingents from Pennsylvania, Massachusetts, Florida, New Jersey, and many more. It was hard to believe that we'd grown from a regional grassroots organization, which may even overstate our beginnings, to one known nationally. And we also knew that we were on the side of justice, and our many supporters recognized that, as well.

We had heard rumors that Governor George Pataki might attend our memorial service. We took this as a significant expression of his support for us and his desire for the task force to be diligent and fair in its dealings with FVOA. Because of 9/11, he understandably could not be there with us.

Within a month, there was further evidence of the strength we wielded. In October, I learned that the State University of New York campus at Cortland was hosting a symposium on prison reform. The university leadership had decided to invite a man whom the faculty apparently believed to be an expert on corrections and incarceration issues. "He is, as I understand it, an author and activist on prison reforms," the university's dean of arts and science said to local media. "This conference is an attempt to look at those issues and broader social issues."

The supposed expert was John Hill. He was then using the name Dacajeweiah, and promotion materials for the symposium advertised him as "a leader of the Attica rebellion." I was furious.

I went to Gary's office, wondering if we had any recourse. Here was a state university hosting the man convicted of killing my father and being hailed as an "expert." Gary reminded me that Hill was a free man and there were no restrictions on what he could and could not do with his life. I was bubbling with anger; Gary was far calmer about Hill's right to make the presentation.

I would have none of it. I called Senators Volker and Michael Nozzolio, telling them about the Cortland program. While there was friction in my relationship with Volker, on this point we agreed: Hill shouldn't be on a state-sponsored panel about corrections reforms.

NYSCOPBA officials also went to bat for me, telling the Rochester *Democrat and Chronicle*, "This man is purporting himself to be the leader of the Attica riot. He's purporting himself to be an expert as far as Attica is concerned. What he really should be purporting himself to be is the convicted killer of a corrections officer."

The university at first defended its decision, saying that it should be a restriction-free forum for opinions, even those that some might find "objectionable." And I had no issue with the agenda of the symposium; if anything, I had become far more sympathetic to the issues surrounding mass incarceration. But surely there were many other experts other than John Hill who could speak on the topic.

It only took a day or two for the top official of the state university system—the state chancellor—to inform Volker that Hill would not be on the panel. He apologized to Volker for Cortland's choice. As I would later learn, Hill was already in a hotel room in Cortland, awaiting the day of the presentation. He was told he was no longer welcome, and, if what I was told was true, the State Police escorted him the two hours to the Canadian border.

The Pains of 9/11

It would be another ten years, oddly again on a decennial anniversary of the riot, when John Hill would again find a way to intrude in my life. The state university, the University of Buffalo, was then holding a day-long symposium on the Attica riot and still-lingering issues of conditions within the nation's corrections system. In some ways, the symposium mirrored the topics raised a decade earlier at Cortland, but the University of Buffalo agenda was far more extensive.

I was on a panel entitled "Looking Back: The Attica Rising and its Aftermath," along with Arthur Eve, Malcolm Bell, Michael Smith, and historian Heather Ann Thompson, who would later write the Pulitzer-winning history of the riot, *Blood in the Water: The Attica Prison Riot of 1971 and Its Legacy.* During the presentation, I received a text message from a friend in the audience alerting me that John Hill was there, only two seats away from her. The auditorium held hundreds, and I could not locate my friend, who was near the back, nor confirm if Hill was in the crowd. Even if he were, I likely would not have recognized him.

In a question-and-answer session after our presentations, a man came to the microphone and specifically addressed a question to me. He told us first of his life: He had been on death row when the death penalty was ruled unconstitutional. He later was freed from prison, and now worked with nonprofit organizations focused on corrections reforms. Days before our symposium, he said, he and others had gathered for a walk to the Attica prison to remember the riot. He had organized the walk and called it "The Walk for Justice and Reconciliation."

I still had no idea why he was aiming his question to me and not other panelists. Then it became clear.

"My question, Dee, is if John Boncore was to come in and say, 'Can you forgive me for what I did?' could you open your heart if he was sincere. Could you forgive him?"

I felt all of the other panelists looking at me. I looked to the front row, where NYSCOPBA's Rick Harcrow was seated. Rick had come with me, telling me he would be "my bodyguard" if I confronted anyone who might be a problem. I was trying to gauge his reaction to this question. He was asleep.

I knew John Hill's middle name was Boncore, and he had used his full name in the past. I asked, just to make sure we were speaking about the same person.

"John Hill?" I asked.

"Yes, John Hill."

I paused again, unable to answer.

"I don't mean to put you on the spot," he said.

"You just did," I responded.

I tried to gather my thoughts. Finally, I said, I was sure there were many people who were involved in the beating of my father. The attack on him occurred, I said, "not because he was Bill Quinn, because he was somewhat well-liked in the prison, but because he had on the uniform.

"I have, through the years, kind of come to a state where I don't really know who did what to my dad," I said. "I just know he was injured very badly and subsequently died two days later."

My statement did not mean I was prepared to forgive John Hill, who I now realized must be in the audience, just as my friend had said in the text.

"I don't really know how I feel about John Hill," I said. "I know how I felt about him as a child, how I was brought up, but my evolution is different than...when I was a kid. That's where I'm comfortable sitting at right now, and that's where I'm going to stay."

I knew if I ever was going to speak with John Hill, it would be on my terms, and not with some blindsided attempt at an apology before hundreds of people. Two years later, Hill died in Canada, after he took a fall and died of a serious head injury.

Charles Pernasilice, as of this writing, is still alive. He once wrote to me in the early years of FVOA. He addressed the letter properly to me by name, then opened it with, "Dear Lady."

In the letter Pernasilice noted that his name had been removed from the list of those Attica inmates receiving restitution, but he knew he was supposed to receive $6,500 from the attorney payouts. He was not happy. "I have been paid an infantile sum for the suffering from the attorneys' fees," he wrote. "I hope you do not lament this fact."

He said that John Hill was solely responsible for my father's death. "I have written you this note in the hopes that you can let go of whatever animosity you are holding against me personally," he wrote.

I did not respond. That was my last dealing with Charles Pernasilice.

Now, a half century after the riot and years after I only knew John Hill and Charles Pernasilice as killers when discussed in my home, I still have no reason to hold them solely accountable for the death of my father nor to excuse them if they were involved (and a jury had found that they were).

As I said at the University of Buffalo ten years ago, that stance is "where I'm comfortable sitting." And I still am. Neither men hold any power over me any longer.

CHAPTER NINETEEN

Shattered Dreams

My mother first saw my dad when they were both sixteen years old. He worked as a bag boy at a local grocery store, and she was immediately smitten. She'd find excuses to go to the store a few times a week.

In July 2002, in "Hearing Room A, Legislative Office Building" of Albany's governmental complex, my mother told a roomful of rapt listeners and the Attica Task Force of that instantaneous spark. She went on about the romance that ensued.

"He was very handsome with dark black hair and big beautiful blue eyes. His long eyelashes and freckles just melted my heart. I knew at first sight that he was the man I wanted to marry someday.

"I went to the grocery store every chance I could, just to see him and hoping he could notice me and ask me on a date."

My father finally did just that, and my mother and he began a courtship that led to marriage and three daughters—one born after his murder.

We were in the second round of task force hearings when my mother served as a witness. We had decided as a family that there would be more power if we were to testify in the state capital of Albany. And we had decided that my mother should be first.

My sisters and I had worked hard to prep her, trying to soothe her nerves. She had gotten more comfortable if asked questions by reporters, but this was different: This was a full-blown testimonial presentation before a panel of state officials and lawmakers. She had watched me speak at many events, but this was completely new for her.

Her testimony was written, as was all of ours, and we told her just to read from the pages. She didn't have to pay any attention to the task force panel if she so chose.

"Bill asked me to marry him, and we married at St. Vincent's Church in Attica, in New York in 1965," she told the panel. "I remember that day like yesterday. It was a bright, sunny day and the temperature was in the 80s, and remained in the 80s for two weeks while we were on our honeymoon in the Thousand Islands on the St. Lawrence River."

My mother led the panel through my father's employment, up until he decided to take the corrections officer test. And she then talked about the start of our new family.

"I gave birth to a beautiful baby girl with Billy's black hair and long eyelashes. We named her Deanne. Bill was very excited with our new daughter, Deanne. She only weighed six pounds and was very tiny.

"She was so tiny that he was afraid if he held her, he might drop her. I assured him he would be all right holding her, and he held her like a fragile little package."

My mother told of how my dad gave me baths, prepared my bottles, rocked me to sleep as he sang to me. For most, this would be the recollections of a standard childhood. But, for us, this was something else: A reminder of how loving and stable and downright normal our world was before it all came to an end. This was what we had, and this is what we'd lost. Come September 1971, we would be a normal family no more.

My sister, Christine, was born in October 1967. "Bill loved his little girls," my mother said. "He read to them before going to bed and we talked about their future often. He even brought them home a dog,

Charlie." Of course, while our Labrador Charlie may have ostensibly been for us, he became my father's playful pal.

It was clear from my mother's testimony that my father was a kind man constantly working to better his opportunities for himself and us. He'd enrolled in classes at Genesee Community College because of the employment possibilities a criminal justice background could give him inside the prison and out. He was so respected within the Attica Fire Department that he was chosen its president. He believed in community service, a trait that would be passed down to his children and then to our children.

I had long come to recognize just how difficult life must have been for my mother, but I'm not sure it ever resonated with me as much as it did as I watched her speak that day. How, after the loss of my father, could she have confronted her grief, taken care of two young girls, handled a newborn, then remarried and had a new child and a new home? I can't imagine how one could navigate that. As I sit and write this, I feel as if I've come to a better understanding of my mother. She raised us girls while operating in a survival mode, grieving her husband and loss of a life they had planned. She lost her dreams and likely herself for a good portion of her life. That makes me sad but eternally grateful.

My mother had rarely spoken to us about those trying and exhausting times. She had persevered. And here she was, having defeated her nerves, about to tell a governmental panel about what were the worst and most unimaginable days of her life. She was nervous, I was sure, but she was heroic.

In the months before September 1971 there was clearly simmering unrest at the prison, so much that my father had helped guide my mother through household expenses and our checkbook, important papers including his life insurance policy, in case something did happen at Attica. Yet no one within the corrections administration seemed to take the signals of forthcoming trouble seriously. My father saw the signs, as did some of his colleagues, but those in positions of power either didn't pay attention or didn't care.

Listening to my mother talk about the injuries suffered by my father was especially tough for me and my sisters, and I'm sure it was doubly difficult for her to describe. But she did. She had decided that, as part of FVOA, she had a role to play and the historical record that would be the byproduct of these hearings would not be complete without a full reckoning of what happened to her husband and to her.

At the hospital, my father's arms and hands were swollen, his head bandaged. He was unconscious, but my mother held his hand for hours, speaking to him, whispering to him, hoping that he knew she was there by his side. Despite the severe injuries he'd suffered, he was still the beautiful sixteen-year-old she'd seen at the grocery store years before. If only he would speak to her, and then heal, life could again be normal.

He never again did speak to her. The scope of his injuries required his transfer from the Batavia hospital to one in Rochester. My mother was told that, if he survived, he could be in a vegetative state. She continued to stay by his side in Rochester.

As she said, she "sat there minute by minute, hour by hour, holding Bill's hand, holding my beautiful husband with love. There were no guarantees. He did not speak to me any time or acknowledge my presence. I talked to him and told him the girls were all right and we loved him and he was doing well."

She was in a hospital waiting area when she saw "a large commotion by the hospital staff at Bill's door." Seconds later she heard an announcement seeking help for a "code blue." Shortly after, she was told that my father was dead.

My mother talked about the agonizing days afterward, as she had to tell us of our father's death, as she lost so much weight that she had to borrow a cousin's dress for the funeral. The funeral itself had largely disappeared from her memory, she said. This reminded me of the photos

I'd seen years before in which my grandparents appeared to be holding my mother upright at the funeral, as if her state were so fragile that she could topple at any moment.

She told of the constant barrage of media phone calls to our home, of reporters' requests for photographs of my sisters and me. She finally changed to an unlisted number. She recalled how she reached out to a local priest for guidance because she thought she was "out of control." She remembered her first Christmas without our dad, only months after his death, as she was alone for the wrapping of gifts that she and my father usually did, joyfully, together. She had to stop. She sat on the floor, with us in our beds, and cried. Amid her tears, she prayed for help, and a neighborhood couple showed up at the door to check on her. They helped her wrap the remaining presents and piece together toys that needed construction.

My sister, Amy, was born eight months after my father's death. A nurse came into the waiting room to tell the proud father of Amy's arrival. There was no father present. Both of my grandfathers were there and explained to the nurse our family circumstances.

"When I held Amy for the first time, with her huge blue eyes, long eyelashes, and dark hair, I knew Bill was with me all through the pregnancy and delivery," my mother said.

My mother reminded the task force that the men convicted of killing and beating my father had gone free. It was another insult.

"When is it going to end?" she asked the task force. "The families existed in poverty and emotional upheaval. Apparently, it looks to me as if more time, effort, and consideration was used to cover up the riot than to help the state's own employees and families."

Years later, when I would read transcripts of my mother's testimony for the first time in what seemed like an eternity, I had to take a break. I began reading them one night before bed, and the ache in my mother's words was too much for me. I laid the transcripts aside, knowing I would not sleep if I read any more. They were no easier for me to read the next day.

I knew what strength my mother had to gather to do this. There were members of FVOA who had chosen to give only written testimony to the task force. Some did so because they doubted the task force would do anything for us; some simply did not want to testify publicly; some lived too far away or were physically unable.

My mother could have chosen that route, as well. But she sat before the panel for a half hour, reliving the most painful days, months, and years of her life. She ensured that the historical record would not forget Bill Quinn, the darling love of her life, the man who'd been stolen from her.

"My husband was murdered and forgotten by our prison and judicial system," she said.

"Bill went to work September 9, and my life has never been the same."

CHAPTER TWENTY

I Thought My Dad Was Superman

As the July 20, 2002, task force hearing progressed, our testimony became both the Quinn family tragedy and the tragedy of Attica as a whole. All of the survivors had their unique and singular anguish, just as we did, but there was a common thread throughout—the sense that we'd been abandoned.

After my mother's presentation, each of the sisters spoke to the panel.

The state had acknowledged the suffering of the inmates, my sister Christine said, yet we, the families of state employees, had been pushed to the side and forgotten.

"I do not have scars on my feet from walking on broken glass," she said. "Or healed physical injuries from the beating after the prison was retaken. I live with irreparable [pain], and I am here waiting for my life. I needed my father then, and I still need my father now."

Like my mother, Christine also told of our special childhood. She remembered our father as a "big, strong, handsome man with giant-like blue eyes, long black eyelashes, and closely trimmed thick black hair."

"I thought my dad was Superman," she said.

After the riot, we had no anonymity, she said. She and I at a very young age would go to the store with the grocery list of what our mother needed, and the clerks were always helpful, stocking our bags and making sure we had the proper change afterward.

But, Christine said, she'd often hear people whisper, "There are the Quinn girls." I was petite with my father's black hair and Christine taller with red hair. We were hard to miss as a pair.

She spoke of how our lives were turned upside down. "I changed churches, and religion, got a second sister, a stepfather, a third sister, moved to a new town, and new house, and went to a new school," Christine told the panel.

Christine, like me, would leave classes sometimes in junior high and high school if the riot was discussed. When asked by teachers whether she wanted to stay or not, it was another blow to anonymity; any students who did not know who she was and her tragic connections to the riot found out each time she was asked.

Christine spoke about the college experiences we all encountered. We all knew the bursars by first name. Our college assistance, through the fund set up for the children of those who died at Attica, was good at State of New York institutions. It was immensely helpful for us, but there were always headaches at college explaining the fund and how it was to be applied. We were on a first name basis with a woman named Melissa, who oversaw the Attica Fund. Thank God for her because no one else could cut through the red tape like she could. I believe she retired sometime after Amy finished college. We remain thankful for her seeing the Quinn girls through our college years.

Christine told the panel how the assistance would wrongly be applied to the state's Tuition Assistance Program (TAP), which had limits. The Attica aid would push total assistance over what TAP permitted, and the school would reject the aid. We'd receive notice that our tuition was not completely paid.

"Every semester during my undergraduate studies I had to...explain that it was a special award that I received because my father was killed in the Attica Prison Riot of 1971," Christine said. "This total stranger did not care, and I always had to go to the Bursar's Office for approval."

More than two decades after our dad's death, Christine began work as a pediatric nurse practitioner in Williamsville, a village fifteen miles northeast of Buffalo. Not long after she started working there, a pediatrician asked if she was Bill Quinn's daughter.

"I am 40 miles from Attica and I still cannot maintain my anonymity," she said.

We three sisters had long decided that we would not let the Quinn name disappear. That is why I kept Quinn as part of my married name, and also the middle name for both of my daughters. Christine and Amy also kept Quinn in their names after marriage and, as Christine told the task force, she named her son Quinn.

"Now I can say Quinn all day and not feel sad," she said. "I hope to say and hear his name as many times as I needed to hear my father's name throughout my childhood."

Amy, who spoke after Christine, had also kept my father's memory alive, naming her son Liam, which is the condensed Irish name for William. Liam looks more like my father than anyone else.

"I am reminded daily of my father when I look at him...into my son's eyes, his big blue eyes and his long, dark eyelashes like his grandpa," Amy said.

Amy was five years old when our mother explained to her some of the specifics of how her father had died. "My mother's intentions were to prepare me for what others knew that I did not and for the questions that they would ask," she said. "I remember crying with Mom when she told me."

Amy told how the anniversaries of every September brought Attica back into our lives but how she experienced it differently than anyone else.

"For 30 years I have been the unborn child, according to the media. It has offended me for years. The reporters used this term as if I did not exist today."

Amy did not hold back on the animosity she felt for the state, saying that what she had learned from FVOA members proved that state officials tried to run from the legacy of Attica without caring for those who bore its burden of hardship.

"With this new information, I have new pain," she said. "I have feelings of anger and disgust towards New York State. The way the widows and hostages were treated in 1971 was underhanded and wrong."

I was the final member of the Quinn family to speak. I was there not only as a daughter who'd lost her dad but also as one of the leaders of FVOA who would ensure that the task force was reminded of our demands and why they were important.

I also wanted the task force to know that its own prison leadership at Attica had done so little to save my father—less, in fact, than inmates like Richard X. Clark had done.

I told how the Muslim prisoners had carried my father on the mattress to the gate. "One of the inmates, Brother Richard Clark, tried to tell Mancusi that one of his own was very badly injured and needed prompt medical attention or they feared he might die," I said. "Mancusi and prison administration apparently did not feel that getting a fellow corrections officer immediate medical attention was necessary. Instead, they were too busy assessing their position of regaining control of the prison."

Christine had told how she had learned that a former prison employee had stepped right over our father to go into the prison. When she learned he lay there unattended and suffering, she could not sleep for weeks, she said. And, as I told the task force, the evidence I'd gathered from firsthand accounts and hospital records showed that about an hour and forty-five minutes lapsed from the time our father was beaten until he was finally taken by ambulance from the prison.

Without FVOA, I insisted, we would not know details such as how our unconscious father was ignored for so long or how his widow and the widows of his colleagues were tricked into accepting workers' compensation payments. I thanked Governor Pataki for creating the task force, and I thanked the task force members, whom I hoped would "listen and learn from our stories."

And, as I reminded the task force, its mission was to consider our demands, which we saw as both vital and reasonable. I then highlighted each.

The apology was "absolutely necessary," I said. "It shows empathy and respect for the families involved and could help restore our faith in New York State's judicial system."

Though acknowledging we did not know all of the records that remained under seal, I said they should be open, archived, and available to the families and public.

The annual memorial service must be written into corrections law, I said. While Commissioner Glenn Goord, one of the task force members, had said he would always agree to the remembrance, we would have no similar assurance, without some legal codification, that future administrations would feel the same way.

Counseling should be available for those who wanted it, I said, telling the task force members that "most of us suffered from post-traumatic stress disorder, which is real and intergenerational."

And, I asked as I discussed the need for reparations, "What is a life worth?" There must be some means to compensate the families, I said, "because it is the right, fair, and just thing to do."

By the time of the hearings, we had developed so many allies of prominence that I chose to end with the words of one of them—Tom Wicker. I read from a column Wicker had written in the *New York Times* in 2000 about the prisoners' settlement.

"In a more lasting sense, the Attica matter is anything but closed. It lives on, settlement or no settlement, a blot on the nation's pride in itself, a terrible if unadmitted example of how American justice can go badly wrong—and not just in New York or in 1971.

"Could it really have happened in this country? It could, because it did. If not admitted, it could happen even again."

CHAPTER TWENTY-ONE

All of These People on That List Are Dead?

Three decades after the retaking of Attica, surviving hostage John Stockholm was doing something he had rarely done before, talking about September 13, 1971.

"You could hear the sounds and the smell of pain and death," he said. "They have haunted me for over 30 years. It keeps replaying in my nightmares. I have nightmares on and off."

Attica has never left him, he said, nor the memories of sitting on the catwalk, an inmate's knife to his throat, sure his death was imminent. Then came the thrum of the helicopter blades, the odors of the gas, and the gunfire. He survived but would forever be plagued by guilt over how he had lived and others had not.

There would be times after the uprising when he and his wife would go to dinner, and he would then drive the babysitter home. Instead of returning to his family, he would then drive aimlessly for hours. He had no destination in mind, no plans for when he would make his way back to his wife. He simply would drive, his mind still clouded by what he'd survived and what others, like my father, had not.

"I would just ride. What I was doing, I had no idea."

All of These People on That List Are Dead?

Traveling from Florida, John Stockholm had agreed to be the very first witness to testify at our hearings before the task force. There would be many more, with two days of testimony at the Rochester Institute of Technology in May 2002; two days in Albany in July, when my sisters, mother, and I testified; and two more days in August.

For each two-day session, Gary and I had spent days and sometimes weeks arranging the testimony beforehand. Many members of FVOA were hesitant, at first unsure if they wanted to be part of the hearings. They had their reasons: Some did not want to publicly air how the riot had affected them and their families, some lived too far away to make traveling easy, some were simply uncomfortable with public speaking, and some still had no trust in the state, despite the governor's creation of the task force and the task force's grudging acceptance of hearings.

I didn't feel I or anyone else were in a position to strongarm anyone into testimony. But we told our members that this would likely be our one opportunity, and that, without our testimony, history would still have no record of what we'd endured and how we'd been treated. We had taken the name Forgotten Victims for a reason, and our desire since our formation was to no longer be among Attica's forgotten.

Some of our members opted to provide written statements, but many chose to testify, with some traveling from across the country to do so. Many wanted an idea of how best to shape what they were to say, so Gary and I crafted an outline for all of the testimony. Speakers would relate their story chronologically. Prison employees who were at Attica in 1971 typically were to tell how they ended up at the prison, then, and this we knew would be the most challenging, to revisit and relive the riot and its aftermath. This was the plan we had for all—a chronology of the lives before the riot, the days of the riot, and the years thereafter, with each speaker culminating with their own thoughts about our five demands.

For many of those involved, the riot was the first step of a descent into hell. Some had confronted alcoholism, depression, family splits, and divorces. Some would flinch or even cower if they heard helicopters overhead. Others, who had been remarkably social beforehand, opted to live much of their lives after in near-isolation, refusing invitations for dinners or friendly get-togethers. Several who had subsequent drunken driving arrests were routed into treatment that they never were offered in 1971.

Some families were even unsure whether the men killed in the retaking had been properly buried. They'd had funeral services, then the bodies of some of the slain were taken away for another round of autopsies afterward. They had not actually witnessed a true into-the-earth burial. Can you imagine being a daughter leaving the cemetery after the burial of your father, only to watch out the back window of the car and see your father's casket being lifted from the ground and loaded into a vehicle and taken away? This happened with one family, and no one ever contacted them when the hostage's body was returned to the cemetery plot.

These were not life stories that our members wanted to openly discuss before strangers and a roomful of onlookers, because the hearings would be open to the public and media. But they also recognized that most of the hardships they'd suffered after September 1971 could be traced directly to the riot and how the state had ignored and duped them.

"I learned that the state considered me, a hostage and loyal employee, totally expendable, but they showed no regard to my family during the days of the riot," John Stockholm said. "They gave them no information, no place to wait, no protection from the weather or the media, and didn't even let them know I was gone [after the retaking] and taken to the hospital. Basic human considerations were totally ignored."

I was the de facto organizer for the hearings. I stayed in touch with our members who were willing to speak, and I laid out a schedule to confirm their availability. Some preferred to testify in Rochester, while I also wanted to be sure that we had speakers in Albany who would, for the media coverage and legislative interest there, give a rounded and complete portrait of the suffering of our membership.

Frank "Big Black" Smith and I had talked about how our roles were similar—his with the inmates and mine with FVOA—and that was apparent as we were key coordinators of the testimony.

At both RIT and in the Albany legislative conference room, I would place myself in a seat on an end of a row near the front so the task force could easily find me if there were questions or any confusion with the proceedings. Still, as much as I was focused on ensuring that all who wanted to testify did so with enough time, I could not help but be moved all over again by the words I heard over those days. I would listen to testimony, then cry during breaks, then return to make sure we continued to have our speakers ready. I listened to every word that was spoken, and it was gut-wrenching, even with histories I already knew so well. My husband, David, was continually worried about my mental and physical health during the time of the hearings. They took a real toll on me. Thank God for my therapist.

And, as speakers continued, I still learned more. I had thought Michael Smith was the only employee who did not return to his job at the prison, but discovered from June Fargo that her husband, Richard Fargo, also could not go back.

"Richard survived the hostage situation physically, but not emotionally," she said.

During the initial riotous outbreak, Richard Fargo was struck in the head with a shovel and a sliver of glass entered his eye from a broken window on a door he tried to secure as he was being rushed by inmates. Taken hostage, Fargo dealt with the pain of the glass shard in his eye as he sat blindfolded in D Yard.

Throughout the standoff, June Fargo, who was a teacher at the Attica Elementary School, received no updates from prison officials about the condition of her husband, though she knew he was alive.

All of the information she received came from television and radio broadcasts.

She lived so close to Attica that she could hear inmates chanting and yelling throughout the nights her husband was captive. "It was chilling," she said. Her minister called her each morning to reassure her with caring words that she never received from corrections officials.

Richard Fargo survived the retaking, but he, like so many others, was never the same. His wife convinced Fargo, a World War II veteran who'd joined the prison system in 1949, to never go back into another prison. He had small pensions available, and he found new work, but his health deteriorated. He suffered respiratory problems, possibly an aftereffect of the gases dropped into D Yard, and recurrent headaches from the blow to his head. He would abruptly awaken in the middle of the night with severe chest pains, and, as June Fargo said, her "calming hands helped him relax." He avoided crowds, always looking around fearfully if he found himself surrounded by a large number of people. He began to drink heavily.

"There were times when I had to be away from home for an evening, or when I was teaching," June Fargo said. "I never knew what I would find when I got home. I literally shook." Her children no longer brought friends over, uncertain of what kind of mood Richard Fargo might be in.

Richard Fargo died in May 1992. "He never got over the fact that his employer could treat him and fellow hostages and widows and survivors so badly," his wife said.

Surviving Attica employees told how the prison had seemed on pins and needles in the days before the uprising, and how, though portrayed as a quick combustible act, the riot had seemed inevitable in hindsight. Some of the survivors maintained that the inmate population had become much more radicalized in the year before the riot, and inmates were aggressively ready to challenge prison policies. There was an acknowledgment among some that the conditions were the cause of the uprising and that the prison management had gone too long ignoring basic needs.

"There were some legitimate [demands], you know, a shower once a week," G. B. Smith told the panel. "I could not have stood that. . . . Once a week, I would have been rioting."

Throughout the hearings, men who'd been hostages in D Yard told how news of my father's death changed the atmosphere. There appeared to be hope for a resolution, but my dad's death made many inmates fearful that they could be criminally charged. Amnesty became a significant sticking point. William Kunstler told the inmates on September 12 that prison officials had agreed to many of the demands for improved conditions, and the offers were likely not to get any better.

When "word got out that Billy Quinn had died...there was a great mood swing in inmates and hostages," G. B. Smith told the panel. "Everybody knew that was a whole new ball game now, and on [September] 12, which was Sunday, things were a little tense out there."

September 12 was also the birthday of G. B. Smith's oldest daughter. "I thought it would be nice if they let me go to the birthday party," Smith, always one to find humor at even dire times, said to the task force. "I would come back later that night, they could hold my spot on the mattress, and I would be back."

After September 1971, Attica became part of the public and pop culture lexicon, though in a way hurtful to those who lived in the community or had ties to the prison. Some of our members complained that Attica, the town, was thereafter not only equated with the riot but also with the worst of the nation's racial bigotry. But while there surely was racism among some of our members, and there were some who did not place value on the lives of inmates, there were many who had worked within Attica who, like my dad, treated the prisoners with respect and received the same in response. The task force heard of these individuals as well.

Though taken hostage, G. B. Smith had been helped by a prisoner who ensured his safety en route to the Yard. Similarly, an inmate had pushed Smith to the ground when the shooting started, an act Smith thought could have been a lifesaver. My grandfather Quinn, a civilian meat cutter at the prison, had been helped to escape by inmates. His wife had long baked cookies for the prisoners.

Colleen Whalen Spatola, whose father was slain hostage Harrison Whalen, told of the articles she'd read through the years, saying of them that "I'd come away with a distinct impression they wanted you to feel like the guards were brutal and they somehow brought this violence upon themselves.

"But that's not a picture of the father I remember," she said.

Colleen told of a family vacation to Mystic Village and Salem during which "we ate in restaurants as we slept in hotels and we drove a lot." Once, sitting in the front seat of the family station wagon, her parents were chatting about an inmate who did wonderful leather work as a craft inside the prison. She still had a purse from the prisoner, she said, one with a long strap and flowers and vines sewn into the leather. Her initials were beneath the purse flap.

Remembering the family vacation, she told how her parents were discussing the prisoner's release. By then, Colleen said, she was tired of the travels and just wanted to return to her own bed. "And I can remember saying, 'He's nothing but an ex-con. Why do you even care?'"

"I can vividly remember my father pulling that station wagon across three lanes of traffic and asking me to have a seat on the guard rail next to the car with him," Colleen said. "Oh God, if I close my eyes, [I] can still hear that whoosh of the cars going by."

There, with traffic zipping past, her father told her how disappointed he was in her. The inmate had made a mistake, had paid his time for it, and now deserved to live the rest of his life without the stigma of his crime, he said.

"How would you like it if I grounded you for something and when it was over, I threw it back in your face every single day for the rest of your life?" he asked her.

The testimony provided other moments like this—powerful rebuttals to the still-existing narrative that all prison employees were hostile to the prisoners, or that, conversely, all inmates were heartless monsters. There were glimpses of humanity, even from the awful days of 1971.

One corrections officer, Raymond Bogart, who was badly beaten, had been helped out of the prison on September 9 by an inmate, Walter "Tiny" Swift, and another prisoner. When Swift got Bogart to the gate, police asked him if he wanted to come out. Swift declined and said he had to go back in.

Swift, imprisoned for murder, had become an aide at the prison hospital, and he returned to the prison to try to help the wounded. After the uprising, the extent of his work during those days became public; another officer said he would have bled to death without Swift's intervention.

Governor Rockefeller pardoned Swift on Christmas of 1971, saying Swift, who became known as the "Angel of Attica," had risked his own safety to help the injured. He died in a car accident in 1973, a day after he was married.

For me, it was the memories of the children of prison employees that I could relate to the most. We all had different experiences, and our own confrontations with trauma, but there was a consistent symmetry in our hurt.

Kentt Monteleone, whom I had grown to know so well from FVOA meetings, was seven years old when his father was killed. His sister, Karol, at the age of fourteen, had answered the phone on the morning of September 13. The call came from an unknown source at the prison, informing the family that John Monteleone was among the dead. During our hearings, there was no shortage of incidents of callousness from state officials, but this was among the worst. John Monteleone's wife was not even at the house when the phone call came. She was at the prison, awaiting word on her husband.

"How could anybody be so insensitive to let a fourteen-year-old know that her father was killed and not have the decency to let their mother come home and tell [the children]," Kentt told the panel. Karol had run through the house, screaming, "Dad's dead," and Kentt retreated to the front yard, where he knelt in prayer.

Like me, Kentt had few memories of his father. Even when very young, he developed an explosive temper. Once, in sixth grade, other boys in the class were speaking of the riot as if it had been "cool," and they then began mimicking the sounds of gunfire. Kentt punched one in the face, stood up from his chair immediately, then walked to the principal's office.

As he told this story, Kentt paused, smiled, and turned to his mother in the crowd. "That was probably one you didn't know about, Mom," he said. "Sorry."

We planned to have some of our "outside experts" testify in Albany because of the media coverage there and the possible interest from legislators who knew little of our cause. Among those we'd asked were Malcolm Bell and Morris Jacobs.

In Albany, Malcolm was fatigued but, unbeknownst to him at the time, he was suffering from Lyme disease. Nevertheless, during his testimony he questioned and challenged the police onslaught into the Yard on September 13, guiding the panel for over an hour through his investigation in the 1970s.

As the man in charge of the possible prosecution of law enforcement, Malcolm knew better than anyone how chaotic and dangerous and, ultimately, deadly the retaking was. There were State Police sharpshooters charged with taking out the inmate "executioners," and some succeeded. But that did not explain the barrage of rounds—more than two thousand—fired into the Yard through the thick haze of gas. Plus, some law enforcement wielded shotguns; the buckshot would spread widely, endangering more men in the Yard. The first wave of State Police were armed with shotguns, a decision Malcolm said may not have been legally criminal negligence but was morally criminal negligence.

"Just all these lethal pellets going out amongst the human beings. I am very surprised that only thirty-nine were killed that morning.

"They killed ten out of thirty-eight hostages," Malcolm said. "They killed twenty-nine out of 1,300 inmates. They wounded with gunfire eighty-nine others. A hostage was fifteen times more likely than an inmate to be shot dead."

Corrections officers were not supposed to be part of the retaking, but some, armed with guns they either brought from home or gathered from the Attica arsenal, pushed through the gates along with the State Police.

Some inmates were shot in what appeared to be deliberate acts, Malcolm said, but the law enforcement killers were, much like John Hill, allowed to escape from their criminal actions.

Senator Volker, again in defense of the state, occasionally interrupted Malcolm's testimony, once asking him why he had not tried to indict inmates who committed crimes during the riot. As was his nature, Malcolm calmly reminded Volker that there was another entire prosecutorial team tasked with the prosecution of inmates, and his job was to see whether law enforcement had committed criminal acts.

While questioning Malcolm, Volker conceded to what we all in the room had known for thirty years: "There were mistakes made," he said. "There is no question."

In his testimony, Morris Jacobs made the compelling case that corrections officials tricked the families of prison workers into unknowingly selecting workers' compensation as their preferred "election of remedy." He also questioned whether Governor Nelson Rockefeller, who had gone on to be vice president and had presidential aspirations, had a hand in the duplicity.

"He was a politician," he said. "He wanted to be president. How would it look if ten widows are successful in suing the state of New York?"

While we had agreed to trim the list of outsiders we'd asked to testify, we did include Dr. George Abbott, who had been an assistant medical examiner in September 1971.

Abbott had chosen to testify in Rochester, and he told of the bodies arriving at the morgue, where they hosed down the corpses because of the overwhelming smell from the gases.

"We had heard the rumors to the effect that the hostages had their throats cut, and that some of them had been castrated," Abbott said. "These allegations were untrue. All of the hostages and many of the prisoners died of gunshot wounds." Three inmates had been killed by other prisoners during the standoff.

The claims that hostages had their throats cut could have arisen from the bloodied blindfolds around their necks, Abbott said. Some may have coughed up blood when shot, he said.

Abbott had assisted the Rochester-based medical examiner, Dr. John Edland, with the autopsies. It was Edland who first publicly revealed that everyone who died in the Yard during the retaking was killed by gunfire and not by inmate actions. That revelation derailed Edland's career and sent him into an emotional and psychological tailspin. He and his family were harassed with phone calls, some of them calling him a "nigger lover." State troopers were among those who would taunt Edland. He ended up institutionalized for a period of time because of the depression and mental anxiety that set in.

"Where is that doctor who became infamous and hated by a lot of people, but really respected by a lot of others?" Arthur Eve asked Abbott at the Rochester hearing.

Edland had died in 1991, Abbott said. "He became profoundly depressed because of all the adverse publicity that he received," he said.

"I think [John] made one mistake, and that was making public the results of our findings by himself," Abbott said. "I think if he had called the State Police and prison administration, and made a joint report of his findings, that things would have been much smoother for him."

Dr. John Edland, I knew, was yet another victim of Attica. In 1971, he had called local Black ministers in advance of his announcement of how the inmates had died. One of them, Minister Raymond Scott, lived in Rochester, and I would come to know Ray, who had also been part of the observer committee meeting with inmates during the standoff. He once told me how he stood next to Edland, as the coroner held a list of those killed by gunfire and told the press of his and Abbott's findings. Ray saw the list and asked Edland several times, "All of these people on that list are dead?" He personally knew some on the list who'd been fatally shot.

Edland may well have decided that he could not trust the authorities to release the truths of the autopsies. As he and Abbott had performed the autopsies, they were sometimes watched over by State Police, who hovered around the morgue workers. The troopers did not like what they were overhearing about the clear causes of death.

In recent years, I have met members of Edland's family, including his widow, Gwen, and one of his daughters, Gretchen. Like me, she is the oldest of three daughters. She has told me of the depth of harassment their family suffered. They would tell friends and family to telephone, let the phone ring twice, hang up, and then call again. This was a sign they could answer those telephone calls. They set up the system because the belligerent, profane, and sometimes racist calls were coming so frequently to their home. Some of the calls were actual death threats, Gretchen and Gwen told me.

Dr. Edland had once given Gretchen a copy of Malcolm Bell's book, *The Turkey Shoot*. The book, and its focus on how officials thwarted

Malcolm's legitimate investigation, apparently spoke to Edland and demonstrated the same forces he believed had aligned against him.

"This is family history," he wrote to his daughter inside the book. "It explains me. I hope it helps you understand why it all happened."

Dr. Edland, like so many others, was present in the words of survivors over the six days of testimony. My father was there, as were the others who died at Attica and those who had passed away in the years since. As taxing as the testimony was for our members, and for me, there was no question when those days were over that they had been worth it. The state had tried to silence us again, and we would have none of that.

In the final day of testimony in Rochester, Kentt Monteleone again came to the microphone as we were preparing to finish. He had a little more to say that he'd forgotten in his earlier statement. He spoke again of the loss of his father and the anger that had lived inside of him ever since. Then he acknowledged just what FVOA had done for him.

He thanked me for the work with the hearings, remarking how he had watched me scurry and dash through the hallways to keep the testimony organized. FVOA, he said, has provided "more counseling" for people like himself than he'd ever had before. Meeting others like himself was its own potent and necessary therapy, he said.

He then again turned to the task force.

"I do hope you guys will help us out," he said. "I really do. I hope in all sincerity you can help us out before it is all too late. And I appreciate you letting me come up and say the things that I forgot to say yesterday.

"And, hopefully, I'll feel a little better, get some sleep tonight.

"No guarantee," Kentt said, "but I have to."

CHAPTER TWENTY-TWO

I Couldn't Stand on That Ground Again

I t hadn't taken long for us to get into the first session of FVOA testimony before I realized how tough it was going to be, not only for many of our group members but also for a task force member, Arthur Eve.

It had been more than a year since my mother and I sat in the Buffalo assemblyman's office in Albany, and he had been so apologetic about what happened at Attica, as if he somehow could have singlehandedly altered the outcome. We recognized the burden he carried during that conversation, and now we were expecting him to hear hours of testimony over six days—four in Rochester, two in Albany—that would return him again to those tense days spent in the prison yard in September 1971.

I had my customary seat for the testimony, sitting on the end of a row. And I'm sure that our members could see exactly what I saw as the testimony proceeded; this was causing unimaginable suffering for Arthur Eve.

Always the gentleman, Eve would politely interrupt when he heard a claim that he had not heard before, then apologize for the interruption and for the fact that he was learning information for the first time. Arthur's face, sometimes weary, sometimes drained, showed vividly that he was committed to being part of this testimony in his task force role but that it would be an emotional battle for him to do so. When too belea-guered, he would hold his head in his hands as testimony continued.

Arthur recognized that the task force's work, even before the hearings, was taking its toll on him, and he asked for another Assembly representative in case he had to move aside. Another Democratic assemblyman, Jeffrion Aubry from Brooklyn, had been chosen as an alternate. Aubry chaired the Assembly's corrections committee, which helped establish prison-related policies, so he was a logical choice for the job. He also was even-tempered and caring, two traits that would help him navigate our hearings and our continued lobbying for our "Five Point Plan for Justice."

After one day of testimony, Aubry found me in the auditorium and kindly asked me, "How are you doing, girl?" I told him that the testimony was tough for me, and he caringly laid his hand on mine. It was just a moment, but a moment that showed me what was in his heart. He was concerned for me and for us in FVOA.

Arthur Eve, like so many of us, had never come to terms with Attica. There were several books written about the uprising, including one by his fellow D Yard observer, Tom Wicker. Arthur had never read any of them. There were fictionalized films and documentaries about Attica. Arthur had watched none of them.

As the first day of FVOA testimony ended at RIT on May 9, 2002, Arthur reminded the crowd that he, too, was an Attica survivor. He had never escaped the riot's reach.

"You talk about the effects," he said. "I almost lost my mind. My wife went through hell with me for six months. I mean absolute hell. . . . That's why I love my wife so much today, because she went through hell."

It was the second day of testimony at RIT when it all became too much for Arthur to handle. As one widow told of how the family struggled with the loss of her husband, she said one son had committed suicide. That was apparently too much for Arthur; he left the auditorium quietly, slipping into a back hallway.

I left also, as discreetly as I could, worried about him. He'd looked like he was just barely holding it together before he left the room. Throughout task force meetings and the separate conversations between the two of us, I knew too well that this was a terrible strain for him. I wanted to be sure he was okay. I could tell that something tremendously emotional had come over him.

I found him in the hallway. He was a crumpled mess, and I helped him to a folding chair. He was weeping, trying to talk to me. I told him to take his time and gather himself. He did not need to say anything.

I knew there was little I could say that would provide him the solace he needed. I gently rubbed his back and shoulders, just to let him know I was there. He was in such pain. I had seen glimpses of the effects of Attica on him before, but this was more than I'd ever witnessed.

He settled some, and I left him to be. Minutes later, he returned to his seat on the panel, apologizing for his short absence. He acknowledged that the mention of suicide had been too much for him.

Despite the emotional turmoil, Arthur did sit through the six days, though there were times when he would leave the panel as testimony continued. I recognized how hard those days were for him. While it was rare, there would be occasional racist undertones to some comments, and one speaker admitted that her son's racist beliefs were directly tied to the inmate uprising at Attica.

But Arthur did not flinch during those times. Instead, his was a sympathetic and empathetic shoulder for some of our members, and he told stories about how he, too, had been misled by state officials while an observer.

He also knew that he and other observers were the targets of scorn from some in the community and in the corrections and law enforcement ranks, he once said. Some thought that the observers, chosen by the prisoners, could not be trusted and were too sympathetic to the inmates. Once, Arthur said, he and Tom Wicker and others were eating lunch at a restaurant in the Attica Village, and the waitress told them that she hoped they all would end up killed in the prison. In another instance, while at the prison, a corrections officer brought the observers a meal and angrily slammed it on a table, sending the food spraying.

The night of September 12, Arthur and Frank "Big Black" Smith had both sensed that the standoff would not end peacefully. Frank walked Arthur to the prison gate and embraced him deeply. They both cried, Arthur said. Arthur next saw Frank naked on a table after the retaking and was told that Frank had castrated Michael Smith—an allegation Arthur could not believe. He later added his voice to those who witnessed firsthand the brutality against prisoners after the retaking.

The lies were bountiful immediately after the retaking, Arthur once told FVOA members at the hearings. Shortly after the retaking, he said, he tried to calm a crowd of protesters in Buffalo, and he repeated what he thought to be true and had been told by corrections officials: All of the hostages had been killed by inmates.

Later, he would learn that was not true, as would the rest of the world. All of the hostages were fatally shot by State Police and corrections officers during the siege.

Arthur had once told me of how he'd spread the lie at the protest, and he couldn't forgive himself for that either. He only said it one time, but he felt that he'd perpetuated it. He could not have known then that what he was saying was untrue, but he could not accept that he'd disseminated something so harmfully wrong. That lie would live on for many years, as many continued to believe the inmates killed the hostages, despite all evidence to the contrary.

Still, Arthur knew his experiences, as traumatic as they were, likely paled next to some of those in FVOA, especially that of the hostages.

At RIT, my uncle, Dean Wright, who was one of the surviving hostages, told Arthur: "Can I say one thing, Mr. Eve? You have explained how you were misled and lied to, and you were in there twice."

"I was in there five days back and forth," Arthur said.

I Couldn't Stand on That Ground Again

"And you just explained how you felt," Uncle Dean said. "That's the tip of the iceberg for us."

"I'm sure it is," Arthur acknowledged.

Years after the hearings, I would invite Arthur to a memorial service at the prison. I would do this each year, and he always declined, but this one time he agreed. He was struggling with health issues, and he told me he'd have someone drive him there.

At the memorial service, I saw him pull into the parking lot with a driver. I waited so I could greet and welcome him. Moments later the car backed up and drove away.

I decided not to call him about it; I didn't think it was appropriate for me to do so. But several days later Arthur telephoned me. He said, "I'm really sorry, Dee, but I couldn't do it.

"I couldn't stand on that ground again," he said.

I told him that there was no need to apologize, but he felt that he'd let me down. He kept repeating that he did not want to stand on that ground ever again.

At our hearings, Arthur's stance sometimes countered that of Senator Volker, who often seemed willing to defend the state, even regarding the retaking. One speaker particularly chastised Volker about a comment he'd made in a television interview in which he maintained that the State Police had little choice but to charge into the prison on September 13. Never during the hearings did he show a willingness to admit that the retaking was an awful, deadly choice. And, once, he questioned whether one slain hostage may have been killed by gunfire that had first gone through an inmate. He was told this was very unlikely because the ammunition would have expanded significantly when it hit the first person it struck.

This would be a dynamic we often confronted: Senator Volker, while working with FVOA, was often an unrelenting defender of the state, while Arthur knew personally the tragedies and losses brought on by the decisions made in September 1971. Yet, when speakers challenged Volker at the hearings, Arthur would come to his defense, saying that Volker was instrumental in convincing Governor Pataki to create the task force. And, as different as they were ideologically and personally, the two were known to work together for projects and programs that benefitted constituents they jointly served.

Such efforts were typical of Arthur. He preferred to find agreement and consensus, while still keeping his beliefs intact. It is no surprise that on the last day of hearings, after Kentt Monteleone concluded his comments, Arthur looked out into the crowd and asked, "Is there a deacon here? Is there a Sunday school teacher here?"

Someone needed to lead a prayer, he said.

When no one offered immediately, someone from the audience said, "You do it, Arthur?"

Arthur paused, then accepted. He asked everyone to hold hands, and we did throughout the college auditorium where we had just spent hours hearing tales of lives lost and lives destroyed.

In a moment of unity, Arthur thanked God for FVOA, for Governor Pataki, for members of the task force.

"We have learned so much," he said, his head bowed. "And we've also shared the pain with many of those who testified here over the past six days.

"Give us wisdom, guidance, and truth, as we try to do your will for those who suffered so long."

Arthur was one of those who had suffered so long, but his heart was now aimed toward doing what was right and just for us. As long as he was on our side, I knew, we had a chance.

An aerial view of the Attica prison in 1971. CREDIT: *Democrat and Chronicle*

A corrections officer at an Attica prison tower, September 1971. CREDIT: *Democrat and Chronicle*

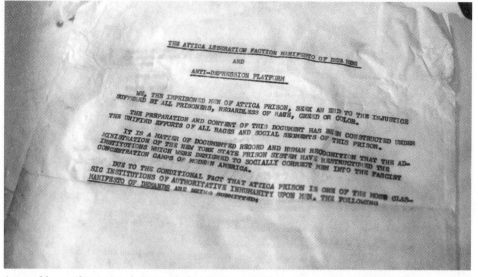

A copy of the manifesto written by inmates before the riot, one of the uprising artifacts held by the State Museum of New York. CREDIT: *Democrat and Chronicle*, Tina MacIntyre-Yee

Inmates at the Attica prison after they seized control of the facility on September 9, 1971. CREDIT: Associated Press

Attica inmates meet with corrections commissioner Russell Oswald during the standoff. Among the inmates is Frank "Big Black" Smith, wearing a knit cap and sunglasses in the center of the photo. CREDIT: Associated Press

State Police at Attica prison during the standoff. CREDIT: *Democrat and Chronicle*

State Police outside of Attica prison before the retaking.
CREDIT: *Democrat and Chronicle*

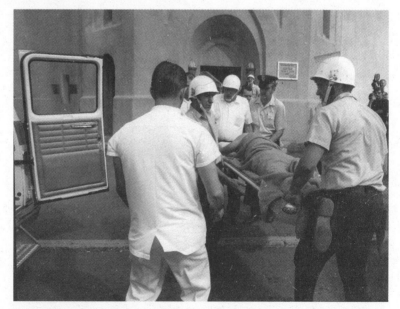

An injured hostage is loaded onto an ambulance after the Attica prison retaking. CREDIT: *Democrat and Chronicle*

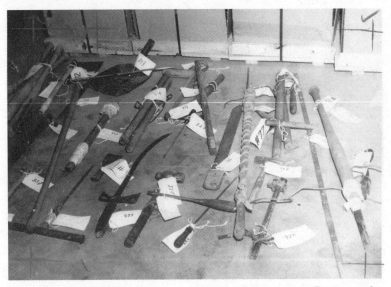

Homemade weapons found in the prison yard after the Attica riot. CREDIT: *Democrat and Chronicle*

The Rochester *Times-Union* edition that won a Pulitzer Prize for revealing that law enforcement, and not prisoners, had killed hostages in the retaking of Attica. CREDIT: *Democrat and Chronicle*

Attica hostage Michael Smith, who was shot five times in the retaking, holds a newspaper with headlines about the riot. CREDIT: *Democrat and Chronicle*, Burr Lewis

Malcolm Bell, the prosecutor charged with investigating crimes by State Police in the retaking of Attica. CREDIT: Malcolm Bell

The memorial placed outside of the Attica prison after the riot. CREDIT: *Democrat and Chronicle*

Frank "Big Black" Smith, an Attica inmate who was tortured after the police assault on the prison. CREDIT: *Democrat and Chronicle*, Shawn Dowd

New York State Police officer J.M. Cason plays the bagpipes on the thirtieth anniversary of the uprising. CREDIT: *Democrat and Chronicle*, Annette Lein

At the forty-fifth anniversary of the Attica uprising, a corrections officer kneels at a memorial for the prison employees killed in the riot. CREDIT: *Democrat and Chronicle*, Mike Bradley

Amy Quinn Miller, my sister, shows her son Liam a photograph of our father William Quinn at an annual Forgotten Victims of Attica memorial service. CREDIT: *Democrat and Chronicle*, Carlos Ortiz

CHAPTER TWENTY-THREE

The Negotiations Stall

After our hearings concluded in 2002, we believed that momentum was ours. The task force had acquiesced, after initial opposition, to holding the hearings in public and having them transcribed for the record. And our members had bared their hearts and souls. It was hard to imagine that anyone who had heard our voices wasn't moved by our testimony.

We knew the task force would not accept our "Five Point Plan for Justice" overnight, but we felt sure that we'd made significant headway.

Then all went quiet. Stone quiet.

For weeks we did not hear from the task force. Then the weeks became months. We began to have a bad feeling that all we'd done had been for naught and that the state of New York was again going to turn its back on us.

We wrote to Governor Pataki, and he referred us back to Commissioner Glenn Goord. We tried to get answers from the task force about what was happening only to receive vague responses that, well, they were working on it. We were told that they'd had difficulty finding times for all to meet, but they were making progress.

The Prison Guard's Daughter

By year's end of 2002, it almost seemed like we were back to square one. But the one big difference from our early days was that we now had corrections unions across the country backing our cause, along with the New York State Correctional Officers & Police Benevolent Association. And the media continued to press Albany lawmakers and task force members about the apparent inactivity of negotiations with us.

A major concern became the status of one of our biggest advocates, Arthur Eve. Arthur decided in 2002 that he would retire from the state Legislature. At his retirement party, which raised money for a nonprofit organization Arthur and his family had set up for the underprivileged, Dale Volker said of Arthur, "It's not just Buffalo, it's western New York [and] the state of New York that he has done so much for."

Thankfully, Arthur asked to continue on the task force, along with Assemblyman Jeffrion Aubry. We hoped there was some movement, and those two were in the thick of it. But we learned from Arthur in early 2003 that Goord and Volker had apparently continued to meet privately without him and Aubry. The task force now seemed to be working secretly without two men whom we considered our most reliable supporters.

Gary spoke with Arthur, who was angry over the turn of events. He expected Goord and Volker to draft some plan, then try to strongarm him and Aubry into accepting it. Arthur said he and Aubry were refusing to sign any task force correspondence.

It seemed as if Goord or task force members had an opportunity to be heroes and do the right thing, but no one seemed willing. And our members drifted back to our initial sentiments about the state: No one trusted them to do anything for us. It all felt like a perpetuation of decades of mistreatment. You have all of these dead state employees and inmates, and nobody wanted to take any accountability. We'd asked for justice; we were getting another dose of injustice instead.

So, we turned up the heat. We created a website and successfully solicited more support. NYSCOPBA placed billboards across the state, imploring the state to accept responsibility. The billboard message was powerful, showing the stone exterior of Attica, proclaiming, "If these walls could talk, they would scream." The California corrections union donated more than $30,000 to our lobbying efforts and flew several of us to Las Vegas for a panel with thousands of corrections union members.

California lawyer Donald Jelinek had also become a partner with FVOA. Jelinek, a longtime civil rights activist, was one of the first attorneys to interview and defend criminally charged Attica prisoners after the riot. Before that, he'd represented Native Americans who'd seized Alcatraz Island in 1969, claiming they had legal right to the land.

Jelinek thought we should bring a lawsuit against the state and that we could overcome the workers' compensation hurdles. But that approach, others advised us, could lead to years upon years of court battles and appeals—much as had happened to the inmates. Many of our members, including the widows, were aging, and we did not want to assume the risk of what could be an unsuccessful and time-consuming litigation.

Jelinek understood, and he offered to help us in another way. He began to file what are known as Freedom of Information Law (FOIL) requests—formal requests for the release of government records held by public agencies—in an effort to unearth Attica documents. Jelinek was game to file a bundle of FOIL requests and to try, if nothing else, to legally harass state agencies into submission.

Later, in 2011, Jelinek released a book on Attica entitled *Attica Justice*. In impeccable penmanship, he wrote in a copy he sent me, "In many ways I learned as much talking with you as much as my research," and kindly spoke of my "unflagging search for the truth." My life, he wrote, "is almost the scope of this book." He died in 2016 at the age of eighty-two.

Occasionally, in 2002 and early 2003, FVOA would get tidbits from Glenn Goord about task force progress, though we knew the entire contingent was not meeting. He once indicated to us that any counseling the state agreed to would be chosen by a bidding process with the provider being the lowest bidder. This was another slap in the face. The state office that assisted crime victims helped with therapy and did not use a low-bid selection. But we were not to be treated the same.

We'd had enough. If the task force was going to do nothing, then we would not sit by silently. Goord had claimed that the task force was working toward a report that could provide some resolution, but we saw no sign of it. He said there was no need for further meetings with FVOA membership until the task force findings and proposal were complete.

We decided to issue our own report instead.

Titled "A Time for Truth" the February 2003 report stated in its opening words, "The Attica tragedy included some of the worst blunders and atrocities ever committed by the state of New York, but the state still hasn't acknowledged its mistakes, which were many and avoidable. Nor has it apologized for its terrible actions, which caused incalculable pain and suffering that continues to this day, more than forty-three years later."

We'd hired Scott Christianson, a historian and freelance journalist who had written extensively of corrections and prison reform issues. He had also helped us create an online version of our hearing testimony, so we could direct people there.

Like so many others, Christianson had his own Attica-related history. He had worked for the state Commission of Correction, New York's watchdog agency that monitors prison conditions, as an investigator after the riots, and he later headed an investigation into conditions at Sing Sing Correctional Facility.

In July 1976, Christianson publicly revealed that, in the opinions of some at the commission, the conditions at Attica then were as bad as they had been in the months before the riot. He was fired afterward, with his boss telling him, "I feel you are a brilliant and dedicated member of this staff [but] it is clear that you intend to work in a totally independent way."

Our February 2003 report was a salvo fired at the task force. As we wrote in the report, Goord "has declined to engage in any further consultation with the Forgotten Victims of Attica."

We did not ignore Governor Pataki either, who had been reelected to a third term in 2002. "Since gaining his re-election, Governor Pataki has not included any mention of us in his State of the State Message or his Executive Budget," the report said. "Other state officials still have not fully opened the Attica files or responded to our Five-Point call."

Our twenty-four-page report summarized the riot history and our five demands. An apology, we wrote, would acknowledge how the state's actions had led to death and injury and would also admit to "the state's duplicity regarding compensation." The opening of records could "provide closure to victims" and "expose the cover-up the state perpetuated." Counseling was needed for those still suffering, and the annual ceremony was necessary for us "to memorialize our family and friends." The restitution, we wrote, would be "compensation that is deemed fair by the victims."

For the report, Christianson drew heavily on the testimony from the hearings. He extracted quotes from the many witnesses, including corrections officer Ron Kozlowski, who said, "I turned twenty-three in the Yard, not expecting to get much older."

Ron, who'd been a hostage, had also testified about the days in D Yard. The inmates "combed my hair and told me they wanted me to die pretty," he'd said. "A little while later, [they] asked me if I was scared. I said 'yes' and [they] gave me a Tums and said, 'Eat this now and don't worry. In a little while it will be all over anyway.'"

Ron had also been taken to the catwalk as a hostage. When the retaking began, his inmate captor's knife had cut across his throat; the wound required thirty stitches to repair.

Christianson condensed the hours of testimony into some of the most harrowing, painful, and anguished comments he'd culled from the hearings, memories such as those of Ron. Some of those recollections came directly from my family and me. The report quoted me saying, "During my father's hospitalization, no one from the state came or called. My uncle Bob was left to call the prison and inform them my dad had died."

Regarding my grandparents, Christianson quoted my mother's testimony: "Bill's mom and dad grew old even faster than expected, as their emotional state deteriorated each and every day. They died without closure to their son's death."

Our report ended with a hearing quotation from Colleen Whalen Spatola, the daughter of slain hostage Harrison Whalen: "Those slain at Attica should not be forgotten. What each and every survivor...lived through should not be forgotten."

We bound the report and sent it to every member of the state Legislature. As expected, we received media coverage, and officials in Glenn Goord's office told the press that a task force report was nearing completion. Months later, when the media again inquired about the task force's work, the response was the same: Its report was nearing completion.

I did have one drop-in meeting with Goord during this time, though task force business was not on the agenda. Instead, it was simply a chance to say "hello" while I was at a NYSCOPBA event in Albany. There was no need for an adversarial confrontation, but I did hope to get some sense of task force progress.

I'd come from a reception and was dressed in a black wool Pendleton skirt and a black printed sweater. I remember this vividly because of the canine greeting in the commissioner's office. Goord was kind to me—he would tell me how proud my father would be of me—but he also had a yellow Labrador named Mogul he would regularly bring to his office.

A friendly dog, Mogul came over and lay his head on my lap as I pet him while Goord and I spoke. Mogul slobbered on my skirt, but I'm a dog lover so it didn't bother me much.

The Negotiations Stall

Then, I noticed that Mogul was wearing a corrections badge. I had seen the badges on other dogs, but they were canine working dogs used by corrections officials to search out drugs in prison cells or other areas. Department of Corrections dogs were named after fallen corrections officers. I once met Quinn, a gray and black-haired drug-sniffing German Shepard who wore a Department of Corrections badge and was used by the corrections agency. His handler, officer Tim Snyder, had introduced me to him and our family. I was touched by the honor given my father's name. I had a tough time reconciling a badge on Mogul.

Meanwhile, our report had gotten attention, and while it served as some embarrassment for the task force, it did not seem to change the equation. We continued to wait, occasionally exchanging emails and correspondence and receiving assurances that the task force conclusions were imminent. The task force definition of "imminent" was surely different than ours.

We'd believed that by the 2003 anniversary our work would be largely done. That was not to be. "I'm just sort of downhearted about it," Ann D'Arcangelo Driscoll told the Rochester *Democrat and Chronicle*. "I just thought it would have been settled by now."

Each anniversary, she said, she has a flashback to the days when her husband, who died in the retaking, was held captive. The memories of the deaths and violence of September 13 are "absolutely horrifying," she said. Every year on that date, "I absolutely get anxiety-ridden."

Frank "Big Black" Smith was quoted in the same article, saying of our group, "I think they're victims. [The state] did it to their own," Frank said. "They didn't have any humane concerns."

Every September is difficult for me, my family, and FVOA members. Some remember September 9 more prominently, especially those who'd worked at the prison and were able to escape or, as happened with some, were helped out of the prison by inmates. For me, my sisters, and my mom, September 11 is the toughest of anniversaries, the day we lost a father and husband. For many, September 13, when so many died at the hands of the state, is the most arduous of anniversaries.

We knew that a resolution with the state could not erase our pain in 2003, but we had hoped for something, for anything. And, again, it seemed as if we'd been dismissed. As we gathered on September 13 that year on the very grounds where so many had shed blood, where so many lives were lost, and where so many families were tossed into an abyss of suffering, we again were among the forgotten.

"My basic goal is just to have my daughter understand her father had worth," Ann D'Arcangelo Driscoll said on that day.

"Not monetary worth. But just worth."

CHAPTER TWENTY-FOUR

Saying No to $10 Million

In December 2004, I took a call from a state official and rejected his offer of $10 million for the Forgotten Victims.

I said no without talking to Gary, without talking to Jonathan or Michael, without talking to any of our members.

And, within hours, I wondered if I'd done the wrong thing. Had I just cost our members, especially our widows, especially my own mother, any restitution? Had I just completely upended and ended our negotiations with the state? One of the widows, the wife of slain hostage Harrison Whalen, had recently died, and others were not in the best health.

Anxiety overcame me. Over the next two days it worsened, and I fell into a tremendous funk. No more calls came from the state or the task force. I had singlehandedly destroyed all of our hard work. Three days after I rebuffed the offer of $10 million, I was taken to the emergency room at our Batavia hospital. As much pain as the legacy of Attica had brought me, and as much as it had cost me, never before had I suffered like this. My heartbreak was inescapable; my guilt overwhelming.

The journey to my hospitalization had been gradual, with much of 2004 in a steady tug-of-war with the task force and the governor's office over our demands and what we would or would not accept.

After the 2003 September memorial service, negotiations had still appeared stalled, with little word from the task force except occasional assurances that we should expect to hear something soon. In November 2003, we finally found out what the task force—apparently minus Eve and Aubry—had been working on. The November 25, 2003, Rochester *Democrat and Chronicle* had splashed across the top of its front page an article headlined, "$8 Million in Attica Offer."

The article detailed a "draft report" of the Attica Task Force with recommendations as to how to meet, or deny, our five demands. Reporter— and this book's co-author—Gary Craig, who wrote the article, did not reveal who had given him the draft but quoted corrections officials saying it was largely the work of Goord based on our demands and task force meetings. The proposal was presented as a starting point for further discussions, even though we had been discussing our demands for more than two years at that point.

There was also another major problem with the draft report: No one at the state or with the task force had given a copy to FVOA before it found its way to the media.

I'd become the go-to FVOA member for media quotes, but I was so angry at learning of this proposal from the press that I referred any media inquiries to Gary. While we knew we would be expected to give some ground on the issue of restitution, Gary pointed out to the media that $8 million did not reach the threshold of $1 million for the FVOA widows, a number that was the logical outgrowth of what had been awarded widow Lynda Jones in her 1982 court case.

Nor did the amount even reach what the inmate settlement had totaled. Goord justified the amount by saying that the inmates received $8 million of the $12 million, with the lawyers receiving the rest. But that did not change the fact that our total was a third less than what the prisoners had been awarded. Gary and Jonathan had insisted that they would take no money from our settlement, despite the countless hours they contributed and our attempts to get them to change their minds.

"The state of New York shot these people," Gary told the media about the report, which largely rejected our demands. "They misled them. They manipulated them for over 30 years and they're doing the same now."

Still, the restitution was not the most frustrating part of the draft report. Once we received a copy, it was clear that the state again wanted to whitewash its actions with Attica. The report did conclude that "there is a plethora of evidence that, by today's standards, reveals mistreatment towards the Attica victims. . . . Under no review of the record can the state contend in 2003 that they have been treated fairly since 1971." But even while acknowledging some mistreatment of our families, the report sidestepped whether the violent and deadly retaking should have been approved and whether families were maliciously tricked into the workers' compensation acceptance.

"To make a recommendation on the issue of fair and just compensation," the report read, "it is not necessary for the task force to determine one way or the other whether individuals were deliberately misled about the effects of accepting workers' compensation checks, whether the state acted negligently in not informing them of the consequences of cashing such checks, whether any of them were given a choice in the matter, or whether state officials were innocently trying to aid them by getting benefits quickly to individuals whose lives had just been shattered, with or without knowing the potential ramification of their actions."

In its report, the task force did acknowledge that pre-riot conditions at the prison were "abysmal."

"Furthermore, the underlying tensions at the facility leading up to the riot were, to some degree, a reflection of the tensions in society at large during that volatile period in America's history," the report stated.

The draft had apparently been circulated to task force members sometime in September, but we'd heard nothing of it. Arthur Eve's comments in the *Democrat and Chronicle* article were a hint that he was not onboard, even though the draft presented itself as the unanimous voice of the task force.

"That was a very confidential document," Arthur said. "Nothing has been finalized."

In its report, the task forced agreed to legislation that would ensure the annual memorial service. But it maintained that any still-sealed records, such as grand jury transcripts, could only be opened by a court order. Any counseling could be funded by our settlement, the report said. And, most maddening, it rejected an apology.

Admitting that warning signs of the uprising were unheeded and that the corrections system was not prepared to cope with the riot response, the report acknowledged state culpability but balked at going so far as to apologize. Our country has engaged in reprehensible policies, including slavery and segregation, but has never apologized, the report said, and "We therefore believe government descends a slippery slope if subsequent administrations believe they have the authority to take their view of today's standards and apply them retroactively to apologize for the decisions of their predecessors whose actions were based upon the prevailing contemporary social standards of our times."

I was furious, and so were other members of FVOA.

Enraged but undeterred, we ratcheted up our lobbying. The corrections unions became more aggressive. Mike Jimenez, the president of the powerful California Correctional Peace Officers Association, wrote Goord personally, saying that California's legislative leadership would have found a way to resolve such a dispute without angering the families of slain state employees. With financial help from the unions, we hired a prominent Albany lobbyist, Artie Malkin, who had been in the business for more than a quarter century. Malkin had once said that lobbyists should push their case with legislative aides and, if necessary, turn to lawmakers' "wives, their mothers, their minister, their rabbi, their boyhood friend—anyone who can have influence."

We also answered with a scathing forty-page reply. We held nothing back. If the state thought we were going to be beaten into submission again and gratefully accept these offers, it couldn't have been more wrong.

How, we challenged, could the task force claim that there were existing standards in 1971 that excused the shooting deaths of ten prison workers and twenty-nine inmates? And how could the state's treatment of our families be written off as if this were the treatment to be expected in 1971?

The counseling costs, we argued, could vary greatly depending on what people needed. If anything, the fact that the state wanted us to foot the bill from our restitution showed why the restitution should be greater. And, while the report claimed that there was nothing keeping many of the Attica records from public disclosure, our requests through public access laws for materials we knew were held by the State Archives had been refused.

In January 2004, New York City had paid $3 million to the family of Amadou Diallo, an unarmed man fatally shot by city police. Part of the settlement was an apology, as I highlighted to the media that were covering our activities. "I personally believe that when there is a wrongdoing . . . what gives people healing is an apology," I told the *Democrat and Chronicle*.

We increased our pressure. I personally wrote to two former governors—Mario Cuomo and Hugh Carey—asking that they implore Pataki to find a resolution. "It would be all too easy for me to hate you for commuting the sentence of John Hill, the man convicted of murdering my father, and pardoning Charles Pernasilice, the man convicted of assaulting my father," I wrote to Carey. "I try instead to understand the situation that you were in politically and personally in 1976."

The Prison Guard's Daughter

In Albany, Artie Malkin, who had greatly reduced his lobbying fees for us, was constantly talking with counsel for Governor George Pataki. As the year progressed, we were as active as we'd ever been. And the schisms within the task force were evident. Arthur and Jeffrion Aubry put out their own recommendation, saying we should receive $15 million in restitution. Each family that had suffered a death in 1971 would receive $1 million, and the remaining would be divided among other FVOA families under their proposal. "I hope and pray we are close because this thing is just being dragged on," Arthur told the media.

The pace of negotiations was a sign to us that we were making headway. I was in the thick of it, so immersed with conversations with lobbyists, supporters, and members that I may not have recognized just how much of a toll it all was taking on me.

Then came the December 2004 call.

I don't even recall exactly who the call came from. I just know that I wasted no time rejecting the $10 million. I then called Gary and could tell he was surprised that I had rebuffed the offer out of hand. I thought I was being a good soldier for the cause because the word we were receiving from our lobbying was that the state might offer $12 million.

The negotiations, which had seemed at frenetic speed before the phone call, seemed to then pause or end. My telephone stopped ringing, and I was left to confront my surging anxiety. I couldn't live within my own skin, and, with each passing hour and day, I became more convinced that I had ruined it all. I languished at home, thinking that I had just lost millions for so many people whom I had come to know and love.

Three days after the call I was in the emergency room at a Batavia hospital, with spiking anxiety and blood pressure. In hindsight, I now know why on that day they considered a psychiatric evaluation for me. I was frantically trying to explain to a doctor how I'd rejected $10 million for families of people who'd been suffering since the Attica riot and I now feared we'd receive no money, and on and on I continued with a stream of consciousness that likely sounded like the rantings of someone with severe mental health issues. I explained it sanely, I believed, but it likely sounded far from sane.

The doctor finally decided to pump Ativan into me through an IV and settle my stress.

Jonathan let the governor's office know I was hospitalized for anxiety. In his inimitable way, he let it be known how tired FVOA was of the endless negotiations. How could you do this to the daughter of a corrections officer—a man who went to work one day and was murdered on the job? he asked. The officer's daughter has given everything she has to this cause, he said, and she is now hospitalized because of the treatment she has received in return.

My hospital stay was short, and not long thereafter the governor's office proposed a $12 million settlement—the same figure as the inmate restitution. I felt we needed to take it. There were only seven surviving widows. I wanted some to be alive to be able to use the money however they chose. It was the least we could do for them.

With Christmas approaching, we did not want to wait until the new year to talk to our members. We scheduled a December 23 meeting at a Batavia church. In a letter to our members, we explained the urgency of the meeting and the need that they attend. We wrote that after December 23 would "be too late to voice your opinion and the group decision will stand."

There was one sticking point that we hoped we could smooth over with our members: The state wanted to pay out the $12 million over six years. The state was in a near fiscal crisis, and we had recognized that an agreement might include such a caveat.

There was grumbling from some members about the extended payout, but we were able to get everyone onboard. We reminded the group that we had been at this for four years, and there were no assurances that more than $12 million would be offered.

The Prison Guard's Daughter

Christmas 2004 was special. We had more to do, but I felt we had succeeded for our members, and especially for our widows. Now we just had to determine how the money should be divided. Who better to do that than the judge who'd done the same thing for the inmates?

CHAPTER TWENTY-FIVE

Restitution for Survivors

In August 2000, as US District Judge Michael Telesca ruled on the amount of restitution for hundreds of Attica inmates, he wrote in his decision, "Just because it is history does not mean it is all in the past. Indeed, Attica is the ghost that has never stopped haunting its survivors—including both the inmates and the families of the deceased guards and prison personnel."

During that summer, Judge Telesca had listened to hour after hour of testimony from brutalized inmates. He heard testimony that convinced him of crimes committed by the police who stormed D Yard, including the claims of an emergency medical worker who saw an inmate, begging for help while prone on the ground, shot in the head by a state trooper.

Judge Telesca, or "J. T." as I came to call him informally, would never forget what he heard that summer, and he would rarely speak publicly about Attica afterward. He and Frank Smith became close friends during that time. On the very first day of testimony, Telesca decided he did not want to hear much from the inmate attorneys; he simply wanted to hear from the inmates. During that summer, Frank organized the testimony of nearly two hundred inmates, and Telesca came to rely on him.

"He was the main contact that I had," Telesca later said of Frank. "I respected Frank because he was one of them, he'd suffered along with them, and he took one hell of a beating. Frank was my liaison."

I'd also developed a relationship with Judge Telesca, who in 2000 made sure that John Hill and Charles Pernasilice were not among the named inmates who would receive restitution. In 2000, after resolving the inmate restitution, Telesca had said publicly that he wished there were something that could be done for our families. We knew we had his support. Throughout 2004 I had occasionally spoken with the judge about how negotiations were proceeding.

Even before we secured the $12 million restitution for FVOA, Gary, Michael, and I had discussed how Telesca would be the perfect person to handle the allocation of any award to us. He had no learning curve, knowing too well the history and atrocities of Attica. I did have worries about how it might affect him. I knew how emotionally draining the inmate hearings had been for him, and I was concerned that it could be too much for him to again revisit the horrors of the riot and its aftermath. But he let it be known to us that he was ready to help if the state agreed. In a private conversation with me, he said, "It won't be easy, but I'll do it."

"I'd like to be the judge who sees this through," he said.

Some of our members were hesitant to accept Judge Telesca, whom they considered too friendly with inmates. Gary and I explained that his role with the inmates was impartial, and he would be the same with us. We spent a considerable amount of time talking to our members about why he would be the best choice. We knew he wanted to get it done quickly, and he would be fair in his approach.

Of course, we ran into some more hurdles with the state. Governor Pataki apparently had someone in mind for the job, but the bigger impediment was Senator Volker. Volker questioned whether FVOA should have an instrumental role in determining the specific awards for our members.

Senator Volker had also been angry that Telesca awarded another $250,000 to Frank Smith, on top of the $125,000 Frank received with the inmate resolution. Telesca determined that Frank deserved the allocation for his many hours organizing inmate testimony and for his work reaching a settlement. It was Frank who once stood to receive $4 million, before the reversal of the jury's decision in his civil case, and it was Frank who agreed to settle the case for far less for himself.

"The record...demonstrates the value added to this litigation by Mr. Frank Smith's special knowledge, factual expertise, investigative skills, sheer force of will, character and determination," Telesca wrote about the extra money he awarded Frank. "Mr. Smith single-handedly saved this case."

In a show of good faith, Pataki had promised that the first $2 million allotment would be in his proposed budget for 2005–2006. We did not want to get hung up over the arbiter of the distribution, so we turned to lobbyist Artie Malkin again. Working his Albany magic, he convinced the governor's office how important it was to us that Telesca be the one to make the tough choices with the distribution of the money.

There was also an unusual pact we made with the governor's office as part of the $12 million settlement: We agreed that a state trooper who had been shot and wounded by another state trooper in the retaking would also receive some money from our award. The former trooper had long maintained that the State Police had done little to address the lasting impacts of his injuries, and he'd left the force without a solid financial future.

Also, and we assume this was not a coincidence, he had been a neighbor of the governor.

In May 2005, the governor formally appointed Judge Telesca to apportion the funding in what had been created as the "Attica State Employee Victims' Fund."

Frank Smith had died of his cancer in 2004, and Telesca knew that Frank and I had also become friends and that Frank wanted to see us get what we deserved. Frank's friendship with the judge had been so deep that Telesca gave Frank a recliner from the judge's chambers that Frank regularly sat in when the two talked throughout the summer of 2000. Frank had loved the chair and often used it to relax with breaks during the poignant and anguished testimony.

As expected, Judge Telesca wasted no time. Within two weeks after the governor's appointment, more than fifty members of FVOA gathered in his spacious federal courtroom in Rochester for him to discuss how best to proceed. I was worried about the judge subjecting himself to more painful testimony, so we agreed that, unless members wanted to speak with him publicly, we would submit written claims. He also had our 2002 testimony to rely upon.

Telesca said that he would take private testimony from anyone who wanted to speak with him. Unlike the inmate settlement, this was not a formal court proceeding, so we and the judge had great latitude in carving out how to go forward.

At our session in the courtroom, where the judge had asked our members to appear to discuss the processing of claims, Carole Butler, the daughter of hostage Frank "Pappy" Wald, told Telesca that her mother might want to meet with him. Wald had survived the retaking physically, but, like so many, was scarred psychologically. In the decade after the riot, he was so overly cautious with all he did that he was constantly checking to ensure the locks at his home were secured. He would look in his car trunk to make sure no one had hidden there. He died in 1982.

Carole told Telesca that her mother was now ninety-three and lived in Warsaw, a small town about an hour from Rochester.

"I'll come out and see her," Telesca said.

"In Warsaw?" Butler answered.

"In Warsaw. I know how to get there. . . . It used to be judges rode the circuit."

Judge Telesca explained to us that he would decide different categories of restitution, just as he had done with the prisoners, then decide where our claims fell within those categories.

"There was plenty of pain to go around for everybody, and we're going to bring that to an end," he told us.

In the weeks after, I told the judge that I did have a concern about a distribution modeled over the inmate settlement. The relatives of slain inmates had received less than those who had survived and still suffered from severe physical and emotional injuries. This was largely dictated by personal injury law, which Telesca well knew because he had been a probate judge before President Reagan nominated him to the federal bench.

I wanted the widows to be the biggest beneficiaries. They had turned down the initial offer of $50,000 for each of them, strengthening the solidarity of FVOA.

Michael, Gary, and I met with Telesca several times about the possible distribution methods. There were some in FVOA who thought the most grievously injured should receive the most, and Telesca helped us all come to terms. He asked that all of our members submit our claims coupled with any affirming documentation to him by mid-June of 2005.

I remembered Frank Smith telling me how some inmates had embellished their stories, and I hoped the same was not happening with a few of our claims. And, as Telesca promised, he heard some testimony privately and traveled to visit a widow.

When all was said and done, we had 150 claims for Judge Telesca to scrutinize. He derived a system to classify them, with categories ranging from $550,000 to $100,000. Fortunately for us, Judge Telesca was acting as an arbitrator for the Attica State Employee Victims' Fund rather than a sitting judge in a personal injury case. With the inmate case, he had to apply inflexible legal doctrines, but he had more independence with our cases.

The judge decided to place my mother's claim in the top category, along with that of hostage Harrison Whalen. He based this determination on the days of suffering for the deaths of their husbands. The widows of other slain hostages received $500,000.

The other categories were $380,000 for those who were severely but not fatally wounded; $225,000 for those who suffered permanent injuries from the retaking, including shooting wounds or beatings by inmates; $150,000 for those who were held hostage and were seriously injured during the retaking or at the hands of inmates; and $100,000 for anyone else held captive at any time during the uprising.

As expected, Judge Telesca had it all resolved before the fall of 2005.

In his order, Judge Telesca wrote, "Although the injuries received varied, the suffering of the family survivors was universal and impossible to quantify....

"Hopefully, the survivors and their families of the Attica riot of 1971 will no longer feel 'forgotten' and that those who suffered and continue to suffer will feel some measure of comfort at least from the fact that the matter is concluded and some measure of justice was served."

We expected quick delivery of restitution to our families, but just as the state was readying to send the first installments, another individual whom we had not heard of filed a claim. He said he had been among the corrections officers who escaped the morning of September 9.

He had not approached us during our years of negotiations, and, as I would learn, he had an unusual connection with my father's death. He had told State Police investigators that he had seen an inmate strike my father with a shovel. As it turned out, and as would be discovered by police, he was lying. He wanted an employee transfer to another prison, and he hoped to ingratiate himself to corrections officials as a witness to the murder. He was willing to incriminate an inmate with lies just so he could go to another prison. He eventually admitted that his claims were a complete fabrication and he'd never actually seen my father on September 9.

As the state was delaying the payments, Judge Telesca intervened in September and told the New York Comptroller's Office that he had been firm about deadlines and that no one who filed a claim after those dates could receive money. The state then issued the first round of checks.

Judge Telesca retired from the bench early in 2020 at the age of ninety. He died several months later. He once told a filmmaker who created a documentary of his life that his work with the Attica victims was "the high point" of his nearly forty years as a federal judge.

Had we received justice? That is tough to say. Nothing would replace what we'd lost or would fully heal our scars.

"I'm not sure what true justice could be in this situation," Gary told the *Democrat and Chronicle* after Telesca's final order. "We're happy we reached this point. Personally, it's further than I thought we'd be able to reach."

The resolution I'd long sought was only partly fulfilling for me. It was a victory—one I'd worked so hard to achieve; so stressful that I ended up hospitalized—but I realized afterward that I missed the constant activity of the pursuit. And while before this mission I wouldn't have considered myself a hard-nosed negotiator, I'd become one. I knew there were officials and legislators in Albany who hated to hear I was on the phone. I enjoyed that reputation.

We still had our remaining demands ahead, but the drive for the $12 million had been constant and all-consuming. Once it was over, I kind of missed it. I'm not sure if it was the loss of the adrenaline rush that retired athletes speak of, but it seemed similar. It was very different not to have that as part of my life anymore.

We connected my mother with a financial adviser for her award. We were practical, paying off the mortgage and car payments. And we encouraged her to do things she'd never done before, like travel to Alaska. My mother had rarely done anything for herself; she'd lived on a tight budget her entire life. She deserved to do something special, as did all of the widows and survivors.

Of course, her award was also bittersweet. She still grieved the loss of my father, the dreamy man whom she'd met when they were teenagers—the man she "knew at first sight I was going to marry someday."

I was glad the restitution afforded my mother the opportunity to live a life she otherwise would not have lived. But she still was without my dad. Does $550,000 compensate for the loss of a human life? Or $500,000? Or $100,000?

The restitution gave my mother and stepfather some financial freedom they otherwise would not have experienced. But it did not bring back my father. No amount of money would do that.

CHAPTER TWENTY-SIX

The Riot Artifacts

B lood-stained and partly covered with a thin dandruff-like coating, the overalls were a stark reminder of the final moments of the life of an Attica hostage. And, here I was, holding them—the clothes that Sgt. Edward Cunningham had died wearing.

Through the Forgotten Victims, his son, Mark, had become like a brother to me. A corrections officer, Mark has always been my go-to person with questions about the Attica prison interior or corrections policies. He has never hesitated to help me.

Mark had not seen his father's clothes, and I wondered whether he should. I had been allowed to open a bag inside a State Museum of New York warehouse that had traveled a long journey—from a coroner's office in Rochester in September 1971, to a State Police barracks, and now to here. Inside the plastic bag were the clothes stripped from Sgt. Edward Cunningham for his autopsy—the bloodied overalls, black nylon socks, and his shoes.

There were dozens upon dozens of similar boxes and cartons in the museum warehouse in Rotterdam, south of Albany. Each contain some relic of the days of the tense standoff and the subsequent violent police assault at Attica—muddied and blood-soaked shirts, homemade weaponry, Bibles, and Qurans.

I wondered whether my father's clothing could be in one of the containers. I had some hope they were. By this point in time, there was very little of my father's life and death that I was not prepared to confront—even the clothes he wore when fatally beaten.

But my instinct told me they wouldn't be here, and they were not. Unlike some of those killed in D Yard, my father died at a hospital. All of the materials at the State Museum warehouse originated from D Yard and the Medical Examiner's Office where hostages and prisoners were autopsied.

It was 2011, and I and other members of FVOA had been in Albany for a panel on the uprising. FVOA had continued to exist and to push for the demands still unmet—an apology and opened records. But, in the years since the state task force resolved some of our demands, we had met less frequently. Still, the Forgotten Victims, through our aggressive and successful lobbying actions and our connections with corrections unions, was now forever linked to the riot legacy. We often were called upon—especially Michael Smith and me—for media or documentary interviews about Attica.

Michael and I had learned about this trove of artifacts from museum curator Craig Williams, who had offered the chance to visit the warehouse and see the materials.

It was Craig who had been notified by State Police that the items were stored largely unprotected in boxes, plastics bags, and garbage cans in an unheated Quonset hut at a State Police barracks in Batavia. The facility was within a mile of my home, and I had no idea the artifacts were there under guard of the State Police.

The homemade weapons and the clothing of the dead, as well as hundreds of other items, were gathered from D Yard and the morgue and kept as possible evidence for the expected criminal prosecutions. All of the items were tagged, in case they were ever needed for presentation in a courtroom. In the Edward Cunningham bag I unsealed, there was a small evidence tag.

State Police told Craig that it planned to dispose of the materials unless the museum wanted some or all of it. Craig immediately recognized there could be historical value in the artifacts. Over several trips, he and colleagues loaded the materials into vans and trucks and transported them to the Rotterdam facility for storage and, as Craig hoped, eventual display.

For Craig, the materials were more than the ash wood of the many baseball bats found in the Yard, or the aging leather of the wallets, or the fading ink upon handwritten letters. These were artifacts of the most violent prison uprising in our nation's history. While they could not tell the entire story of Attica, Craig saw them as a foundation for an exhibit that would bring many voices and opinions and perspectives to the Attica narrative.

Some may shy from the history of a catastrophe like Attica. Craig, instead, saw the museum as an institution that must, as he would say, "bear witness" to the past—even a past that can be particularly painful, and even if the state of New York should not only bear witness but bear some responsibility for the suffering intertwined with that history.

Craig Williams also recognized that the members of FVOA might want to see and have returned to us some of the materials found in the Quonset hut. This was a thoughtful and kindhearted consideration, but it likely helped end Craig's career as a State Museum curator who was well-known and respected in professional circles. Craig Williams would become, in a very different way, another victim of Attica.

The museum inventoried the artifacts and found there were more than two thousand individual items left unprotected at the barracks. As Craig would later tell, there was other evidence stored in the Quonset hut. It included bundles of marijuana with an aroma that couldn't be missed while the Attica materials were being packed up for the journey to the State Museum warehouse.

With the Attica relics, there were hundreds of pieces of makeshift weaponry, including Molotov cocktails and dozens of trashcans filled with baseball bats; letters penned in Spanish from inmates to loved ones; and what may be the lone surviving copy of the inmate "manifesto" that included the prisoner demands.

One item I found particularly heartbreaking was a spiral notebook filled with messages penned by inmates after they were returned to cells on September 13. Some of the messages were simple; some more expansive. They had written notes to let their wives and parents and children and siblings know they were okay. Prison officials were supposed to use the notebook to contact inmate families. Instead, it ended up deteriorating in a box at a State Police barracks, forgotten for forty years.

At different times in 2011 and 2012, Craig allowed some members of FVOA—me, Michael and Sharon Smith, and Jonathan and Gary—to visit the artifacts. Others were also given access: Malcolm Bell, historian Heather Ann Thompson, and Rochester-based documentary filmmaker Christine Christopher, who was then completing a film on Attica.

Heather, whom I was assisting with research for her history of Attica, would later say of the artifacts: "To see those bloody clothes and personal belongings of the corrections officers and prisoners killed by troopers just moldering there in boxes and knowing that state officials never even bothered to return them to their loved ones, and to see how viciously the cells had been tossed—prisoner photographs ripped up and books shredded well after full control had been established—was all so heartbreaking."

That year of 2011, Craig Williams had envisioned an eventual museum exhibit on the riot which would incorporate the artifacts and oral histories.

The Riot Artifacts

The exhibit that Craig imagined a decade ago has yet to happen. The museum had planned an exhibit for the fiftieth anniversary of the uprising in 2021, but that has been sidelined by the COVID-19 epidemic. Still, why would preparations for an exhibit take a decade to begin with? Because, in my opinion, some in state government still refused to come to terms with the deadly wrongheaded decisions made by their predecessors in 1971 and did not want an exhibit at the state's jewel of a museum to stand as a reminder.

Craig Williams was not among those who wanted to close the books on Attica, and to this day we in the Forgotten Victims are grateful that he wasn't.

Some of Craig's superiors at the museum decided that he should not have allowed the access to the artifacts. Some, according to Craig, saw the materials more as an embarrassment to state government than revelatory physical connections to an ugly chapter of New York history. Craig pushed back, trying to get momentum for an exhibit that other colleagues at the museum—those who know that history is not always a pretty story—also supported. As Craig later wrote in correspondence with the museum's top administrators, "Our role should be to preserve and make accessible this material, not deny it or restrict it. We have an obligation to history to make this material available as quickly and completely as possible without bias."

For Craig, the internal fights over the artifacts became so intense that one of his superiors insisted that he also be part of any telephone calls between Craig and me. One of those calls got so heated, fueled by my anger about the restrictions placed on the artifacts and the uncertainty of their future, that I lit up Craig's boss. He tried to end the phone call a few times, but I would not have it, and I continued to let him know just what I thought in language perhaps uncommon in the hallowed museum halls. Afterward I told Craig that what I'd said had nothing to do with him, but I was tired of being treated like a second-class citizen.

As Craig became more unsure of what the fate of the artifacts would be, he took it upon himself to return the wallet of slain hostage Harrison Whalen to his family. Inside was a photo of Whalen's children at their age in 1971. Craig was, as he would later tell us, "severely reprimanded" for his decision to give the wallet to the Whalen family. He still returned some other articles, including a uniform hat worn by my uncle Dean, who'd been a hostage. He was happy to have the hat back, even in its poor condition. Craig also occasionally photographed some of the items and sent me the pictures to see if we could identify whom they belonged to.

In 2014, after the museum blocked public access to the artifacts, Craig retired—a decision prompted by the continued rifts he had over Attica. He also spoke with the media, and news stories popped up around the country about the artifacts. "It's a heartbreaker," Craig told Gary Craig of the Rochester *Democrat and Chronicle*. "This is the antithesis of what I as a curator have tried to do over the last 30 years."

But Craig Williams's efforts resonated in many ways. Heather Ann Thompson and Christine Christopher were helping each other with their projects—Heather's *Blood in the Water* and Christine's documentary—and they visited the artifacts together. In her Attica history, Heather wrote, "Together we just stood for a while, staring at rows and rows of cartons, boxes, bags, and crates of materials that had been removed from the prison 40 years before. And what had been gathered and hidden away for those many decades turned out to be grim indeed."

It was with Christine's documentary, however, that a significant part of Attica history was rewritten, partly because of what she found among the artifacts.

In 2013, Christine and her filmmaking partner, David Marshall, released *Criminal Injustice: Death and Politics at Attica*, which I was asked to help narrate. That film raised questions about whether the

Nixon administration had forewarning of the retaking, and also challenged the official version of the death of one of Attica's most notorious inmates, Elliot "L. D." Barkley.

Barkley, like Richard Clark, had been chosen by inmates to be a spokesman during the days of standoff. He delivered fiery and impassioned speeches that some state officials thought did more to build tension within the Yard than relieve it.

Using official autopsies, the McKay Commission had reported that Barkley was fatally shot in the back by a ricocheting bullet. Arthur Eve had long been skeptical of this version; he said he was allowed in the Yard shortly after the retaking ended and saw Barkley alive.

Among the materials at Rotterdam were the clothing of L. D. Barkley. Christine, through her investigative research, was questioning the official version of Barkley's death. She and Heather had received copies of the Attica autopsies through an unusual source: A relative of Dr. John Edland's secretary had contacted Heather after seeing an opinion piece Heather had written for the *New York Times* about Attica. The secretary had kept the autopsies, and her relative provided them to Heather and Christine.

Christine saw details in Barkley's autopsy that made her wonder about the "yawing" bullet theory—a belief that the bullet ricocheted. She then reached out to Dr. George Abbott, the retired coroner who had assisted in the Attica autopsies and spoke at our 2002 task force hearings. Abbott had been the first to perform an autopsy on Barkley.

What Christine had was the original autopsy, and Abbott said it showed him that Barkley was shot in the back at very close range. There was a second round of autopsy reports by coroners brought in from New York City to check the original autopsies of Abbott and Dr. John Edland. It was possible, Abbott said, that the second report mistook some excised flesh from the wound as the sign of a bullet coming in at an unusual angle, as if ricocheting.

At the museum warehouse, Christine found Barkley's bloody shirt, and the bullet hole in the back was that of a small, straight-on entry. Christine had also found an Attica inmate who said he saw Barkley, lying on the ground in D Yard, shot in the back by a state trooper standing over him.

The new evidence prompted Malcolm Bell, who as a prosecutor had accepted that Barkley was killed by a ricochet, to change his mind. "I accepted the yawing bullet theory," he told Gary Craig. Speaking of the revelations in the film from Christine and David Marshall, Malcolm said, "I think it's a tribute to the residual success of the cover-up."

Most importantly, Craig Williams's concern for the history of the artifacts and our personal connections to them prodded New York corrections officials to take control of the items from their former employees and plan a return. Museum and corrections officials insisted this was their intention and a reason to halt access to the artifacts, but this surely would not have happened without Craig Williams.

On September 13, 2014, FVOA members gathered at the QWL before an afternoon remembrance ceremony at the prison. We had blocked off an area where seventeen stylishly designed oak boxes sat on tables. Engraved upon the boxes were the names of men who had worked at the prison in September 1971; some of them had survived, while some had not.

Corrections officials had found items from the seventeen men among the artifacts and had delivered them to us for return. In the hours before the ceremony, our members went into the isolated area at QWL and picked up their boxes. Some families decided they did not want the boxes, and they left them there.

Through the years, I have heard hundreds of hours of memories and stories and anecdotes from Attica families. We have shared our trauma in a way often cathartic. There is a commonality with our pain, yet we also have our own individual approach to harnessing that very pain.

Perhaps nowhere was this as evident as with the return of the artifacts.

Surviving hostage Raymond Bogart, who'd been helped to safety by an inmate, received his badge. It was sparkling clean on its front and still stained with splotches of his blood on the back. Happy to get the badge back, he joked at how it was appropriately numbered unlucky thirteen.

The family of hostage Richard Lewis, who was severely beaten during the uprising then fatally shot in the retaking, received a box with some of his clothing. The box included shoes that had been too large but were what he'd been given by inmates to wear in D Yard.

Lewis's family did not keep the clothing. Instead, they burned it. Mark Cunningham and his family did the same thing with a bonfire consuming his father's clothes.

Craig Williams also came to the September 13, 2014, memorial service, pleased to see the return of the items to families. The families should be the ones to decide how best to preserve—or destroy—the materials, he knew.

That was almost a decade before this writing, and as I drove along the New York State Thruway returning home from the museum warehouse, my lips became numb, and my fingers started tingling. I felt I was either suffering an epic anxiety attack or something was making me physically ill. I stopped at a rest area where I got sick.

The next day, I spoke with Craig, and we wondered if the residue of the gases still could have been present on the clothing. Not only had I held the clothes of the slain, the attire they'd been wearing when they'd experienced their final thoughts and final minutes, but I also may have inhaled the same gases.

In the past two years, I have met with some of Craig's successors as curators at the State Museum. I let them know upon our first meeting that I had an inherent distrust of museum management, given my past experience—a continuation, I thought, of callous treatment from the state.

However, the exhibit, which is still expected to be completed post-COVID, is in the hands of two people sincere about creating a display that does not try to sanitize the Attica history. I have often spoken with the two—Museum Chief Historical Curator Jennifer Lemak, with whom I share a love for wedding dresses of past eras, and Museum Senior Historian and Curator Aaron Noble. I have faith that the exhibit Craig Williams once foresaw will finally happen.

I've come to believe, after working with both of them, that it is a new day at the museum and there is an openness to understanding the different perspectives on Attica, an openness not previously there.

At least I hope this is the case. Time will tell.

CHAPTER TWENTY-SEVEN

Opening the Records

E ven before we had secured the $12 million in restitution from the state, we were pushing to have Attica records unsealed. We shouldn't have been surprised that, again, there were people who just wanted us to go away.

Michael Smith had begun filing Freedom of Information Law requests for State Police reports, some related to the ballistics findings that would show the different firearms used in the retaking. He was routinely denied.

Working with the task force, we arranged meetings with officials at the State Archives, the repository of many of New York's historical records. There, Attica records from various agencies were brought for storage and, per the task force's instructions, made available for our review as long as the records were permissibly open under state laws.

We set up a formal process for our visits. We'd ask for particular boxes that we were led to believe had certain records we were interested in reading. We'd then set up a date and time for the State Archives visit. I would often arrange for someone to watch our daughters, knowing that we would leave early in the morning and return well into the evening.

Rarely did our visits go as planned.

First, we were treated as if we were going through preflight TSA inspections, as we were patted down and told we could not even take pencils into the room where the boxes would be waiting for us on a table for review. There were fears that the records might be marked up. I had to leave my purse outside.

That was an annoyance, for sure, but it paled in comparison to what was the bigger problem: The archives rarely gave us the materials we sought. Once we were given a box that had three sheets of paper and a palm-sized rock—yes, a rock. I have no idea if the rock was a paperweight or some Attica riot relic that had been classified as an official record.

Other times we would get boxes that did have documents but not the ones we'd asked for. We'd been given an inventory, and would specify what box we wanted, and then we were told that somehow the records had ended up misplaced by previous visitors or had been misfiled.

This all happened during scheduled visits, and I got very prickly with the staff there, reminding them how far we'd traveled only to fail to review what we'd wanted to review. Many times, the staff made it difficult for us to even schedule a time to visit. Trying to make appointments was a nightmare. It was clear to us that they were stalling, hoping we'd give up. We were expected to beg for assistance as if they were going out of their way to do us favors. We were expected to be overly grateful even when we were unable to see a single document we'd hoped to see. It was yet another instance of obstinance from the state.

We also learned that historians Heather Ann Thompson and Theresa Lynch—both university professors on corrections and penology—had been given access to the Attica records at the State Archives with none of the obstruction we faced. One went to the archives before our visits and reviewed some of the very documents we wanted to see, and one did so after. Yet, in between, we were unable to access those very records.

Opening the Records

Our members with the Forgotten Victims of Attica had been eager to see the opening of Attica records. Those who lost loved ones thought that the records, including those from Malcolm Bell's stymied prosecution, might reveal more about the deaths in D Yard.

There was a long and twisted history here, one that made it difficult to figure out where all of the records even were. After the retaking, Governor Rockefeller had ordered the state attorney general to supersede the Wyoming County district attorney with criminal investigations. The Attorney General's Office then pursued criminal charges against inmates and law enforcement officials, with Malcolm overseeing the latter. Malcolm had resigned when he became convinced that the state did not truly want criminal charges leveled against police and corrections officers, and he went public with his allegations.

Malcolm's whistleblowing prompted another probe into the uprising and into the subsequent investigations. This investigation was headed by a former state judge, Bernard Meyer, who was tasked with determining whether there had been, as Malcolm was convinced, a cover-up.

In October 1975, the Meyer Report, as it has been called, was completed. Its three volumes spanned nearly six hundred pages. In the report, Meyer seemed to push right up to proclaiming a cover-up, then stopped short. He said that prosecutions had been "imbalanced" against inmates and said there was a "one-sidedness" to the choice of what criminal allegations to pursue. But in the end, he determined there was "no intentional cover-up in the prosecution."

The conclusions were all contained in the 130-page first volume. The second and third volumes, which included testimony before grand juries, were sealed. They remain almost entirely sealed to this day, despite two different appointed Special Attorneys General—Meyer and Alfred Scotti—recommending that they be released. As long as they were sealed, Meyer and Scotti said, the public would question whether there were uncomfortable truths still hidden about Attica. We in FVOA felt the same way.

There was a widely held belief persisting for years, that Governor Carey, as part of his pardons and commutations, ordered that Attica records be sealed for fifty years. We had Jonathan and Gary look into it, and they found it wasn't true. And Goord in his research found the same thing, saying in the task force draft report that "we find no records sealed by any Governor specifically because they relate to the Attica riot or its aftermath."

Through the years there have been attempts to release the two Meyer Report volumes, but courts have rejected the legal actions, saying that grand jury testimony should remain sealed. Grand juries are secret proceedings, and their records have typically remained closed to the public.

Many records did become public through the inmate litigation, but they were not easily accessible. In Albany, they were kept by the Attorney General's Office, which had defended the state against the Attica inmate lawsuits. The Attorney General's Office held hundreds of thousands of pages in dozens and dozens of boxes.

Michael, Gary, and I would sometimes meet with officials in the Attorney General's Office to discuss how we could review their documents. During one visit, the many boxes were stacked from floor to ceiling in a hallway. In the middle of our meeting, I excused myself, saying I had to go to the restroom. I had different intentions. I planned to go snooping.

I went to the boxes and found one filed with the letter "H." I was looking for anything I could find about John Hill. I didn't see anything on file headings that led me to think there was Hill information there, so I closed it and found another with the letter "Q." I was hoping there may be something there about my dad. I didn't get very far. A secretary caught me and asked what I was doing. I claimed I was en route to the restroom. I asked her where it was.

When I returned to our meeting, I quietly informed Gary and Michael that I'd been nabbed trying to peek into the boxes. I don't think Gary was too pleased, but I think Michael would have given me a high five if he could have.

After the $12 million settlement, we continued to meet with the Attorney General's Office, and Jonathan continued to pressure lawmakers for the opening of all records and an apology. We got an attentive ear with Attorney General Eric Schneiderman, who in 2013 filed a legal motion asking for the opening of the sealed volumes of the Meyer Report.

"It is important, both for families directly affected and for future generations, that these historical documents be made available so the public can have a better understanding of what happened and how we can prevent future tragedies," Schneiderman said then.

One of his assistants, Executive Deputy Attorney General Marty Mack, told the media, "The need for disclosure of the complete report, which analyzed the claim of a cover-up of one of the most infamous criminal investigations and prosecutions in American history, is compelling."

FVOA was grateful for Schneiderman's efforts, but we knew it would be an uphill climb for him. We were not surprised when the union representing State Police filed motions opposing the release. "Grand jury testimony is secret," union President Thomas Mungeer told the *Democrat and Chronicle*. "There's no asterisk that carves anything out. There's nothing in [the law] that says 'historical significance' or anything else and that's the bottom line."

Corrections unions supported the release, and Malcolm wrote a compelling plea to state Supreme Court Justice Patrick NeMoyer, the presiding judge with the litigation, also supporting unsealing. Malcolm proposed a compromise, with redactions of names and any specific information that could identify the accused and witnesses. Such an approach is not uncommon with government records. Government agencies, citing privacy concerns, often redact similar information with records released through Freedom of Information requests.

In April 2014, NeMoyer ruled in favor of a partial release of records but decided that much of the grand jury materials must stay sealed. "If the public's right to know could be a paramount or overriding consideration here, there would not exist a general rule of secrecy in the first place," he wrote in his ruling.

The Attorney General's Office was charged with deciding what could and could not be released under his ruling. That took a year, and in May 2015 more Attica records became public—all of forty-seven pages.

Though limited, those forty-seven pages still reinforced what we knew so well about Attica, providing more evidence of the brutality against inmates.

There was testimony from a local physician who was allowed on prison grounds after the retaking and found badly injured prisoners, including one likely suffering severe brain damage. The State Police refused to let him secure transport for the inmate to a nearby hospital. The physician saw other inmates, some with fractured bones and others in dire need of blood transfusions, being ignored.

A National Guard soldier in D Yard after the retaking saw "guards beat inmates on medical carts with clubs, saw a prison doctor pull an inmate off a cart and kick him in the stomach" and heard a civilian "who appeared to be in charge" refuse to allow a National Guard physician to "set up a field hospital on prison ground."

With the release of the records, Executive Deputy Attorney General Marty Mack said, "Today, we are shining new light on one of the darkest chapters of our history. We hope that, with the release of the Meyer Report, we can bring the families of Attica uprising victims closer to closure and help future generations of Americans learn from this tragic event."

Opening the Records

We felt that FVOA had made headway, but there still was some distance to go. Much of Meyer's two volumes remained sealed. The Attorney General's Office could have appealed NeMoyer's decision, but it chose not to do so because it wanted to expedite the release of some records.

Many did not know in 2015, when those forty-seven pages were released, what I knew: There was a chance more sealed information would become public within the next few years. I had been in close contact with Heather Ann Thompson during her research for her Attica history and had given her full use of my FVOA files. Heather had told me that she had once been accidentally allowed access to some of the sealed records.

Heather spent more than a decade researching her book and in 2004 and 2005 had tried to sort out how many agencies and courthouses held Attica records. She was constantly on the telephone, talking to court clerks across western New York and in Albany. In one call with an Erie County court clerk, she learned that many Attica records had been moved to a room there after possibly suffering water damage. She hurried to Buffalo to determine just what she could find.

"When I walked into that dim file room at the courthouse I was taken aback," Heather wrote in *Blood in the Water*. "In front of me, in complete disarray on the floor-to-ceiling metal shelves, were literally thousands of pages of Attica documents. In this mess was everything from grand jury testimony, to depositions and indictments, to memos and personal letters. Most stunningly, though, I found in this mountain of moldy papers vital information from the very heart of the state's own investigation into whether crimes had been committed during the rebellion or the retaking of the prison...."

"I took as many notes as I could take and xeroxed as many pages as they would let me, and, finally, had much of what I needed to write a history of Attica that no one yet knew."

That motherlode of information became a foundation of Heather's 2017 Pulitzer-winning history, in which she revealed the names of some State Police who were suspected of serious violent crimes in the retaking—the very men Malcolm Bell had been trying to prosecute.

Many of the pages that Heather saw still remain sealed, but, as I write these words in 2021, there is talk of a bill in the New York State Legislature to open them and all other Attica-related records.

Marty Mack and the legislators who want to introduce a bill—and there is a likelihood this fight could be over even before the publication of this book—have asked me to show my public support. They will have my support on this bill because I believe there should be as much transparency regarding the records as possible.

CHAPTER TWENTY-EIGHT

Seeking an Apology

Right up until his death of pancreatic cancer, Jonathan Gradess, the New York State Defenders Association Executive Director, was pushing the state for an apology for its actions at Attica.

Jonathan died in October 2019 at the age of seventy-two, and it was typical of his indefatigable ways that he would not give up. Jonathan was all about truth and reconciliation; he saw it as a path to healing.

I agreed with him, and sincerely thought, even in the early days of the Forgotten Victims of Attica, that the apology would be a demand most likely agreed to. I did not imagine a world in which government leaders could not recognize the calamitous and deadly errors of Attica or could recognize them yet decide the state had no reason to apologize.

As we approach the fiftieth anniversary of the uprising with this writing, we have worked with four gubernatorial administrations—Pataki, Eliot Spitzer, David Paterson, and now Andrew Cuomo. We have met with high-ranking officials in all of the administrations—and still do—yet constantly confront this unbudging attitude that one administration cannot apologize for the mistakes of another.

Jonathan saw the good in a restorative justice approach. Central to restorative justice can be an apology. It can be difficult, bringing a perpetrator and a victim together, yet that reconciliation can be powerful. I watched Jonathan work his magic sometimes, finding ways to unite factions—he even did it within our group when there were schisms—and he always hoped he could do the same with the state and the Forgotten Victims of Attica.

Jonathan would often think we were close to getting an apology. He was eternally optimistic. Gary, the more pessimistic of the two, was always the doubter. Gary's pessimism has clearly been justified.

Through the years we have even passed language back and forth with gubernatorial offices, including the office of current Governor Cuomo. But the language the state prefers is always wishy-washy and equivocal, or so legalistic in its approach to an apology—as if there is still some fear of state liability—that it is meaningless. There would be times when I would be excited to know a proposed apology was coming, and then it would be so watered down that it wouldn't mean anything to anybody.

Never have the proposals reached any wording that simply says, "We're sorry."

In 2004, we proposed this: "The State of New York acknowledges errors in judgment in the handling of the 1971 Attica Prison Uprising and its aftermath which contributed to death, physical injury, psychological damage and denial of just compensation to the Forgotten Victims of Attica."

That went nowhere.

In 2011, we proposed this language with Governor Cuomo: "Because the events that occurred at Attica Prison in September of 1971 caused harm and pain both physical and emotional to the Forgotten Victims of Attica and because in the aftermath of those events these people were mistreated by the State of New York, I, Andrew Cuomo, as the Governor and a citizen of the State of New York apologize for the mistreatment and hurt done to you and your families."

Now, a decade later, Andrew Cuomo is still governor, and we are still without an apology.

The task force draft report from Glenn Goord spent two pages and eighteen paragraphs tackling the issue of an apology.

"There is a plethora of evidence that, by today's standards, reveals mistreatment by the state toward the Attica victims," the report said. "Regardless of whether the mistreatment was accidental or intentional, the result of gross negligence, the result of simple negligence, or the combined product of poor judgment, misinformation, terrible planning and bad luck, the pain and anguish suffered by these victims was nevertheless real and unfathomable. Under no view of the record can the state be convinced in 2003 that they have been treated fairly since 1971."

Yet the state could not apologize. Had Arthur Eve had his way, it would have done so.

Instead the task force report invoked the "slippery slope" argument and questioned whether the standards and protocols of a past era could be the focus of a present-day apology.

Apparently, there was a standard that you could kill your state employees and not apologize. My dad is dead and is never coming back, and the state has the gall to say he may have died because of the norms of the past. What kind of moral fiber are you lacking when you say something like that?

In a 2011 op-ed for the Albany *Times-Union*, Jonathan Gradess and Gary Horton wrote: "Ohio Gov. Richard Celeste apologized for the Kent State killings. Alabama Gov. George Wallace apologized for resisting desegregation. Former South African President F. W. DeKlerk apologized for apartheid, and Nelson Mandela, also a president of South Africa, apologized for the excesses of the African National Congress.

"Apologies release toxins that build up in long-standing disputes; they reveal a common humanity and they begin to repair the torn fabric of community. Many of these apologies and scores of others reflected in history came years after the terrible events had occurred. What they all have in common is that none were too late."

None were too late. As Jonathan and Gary wrote, it is never too late to apologize.

Now, in early 2021, we are approaching the fiftieth anniversary of Attica. There are forthcoming documentaries—including one from Showtime and one in the United Kingdom—that will focus on the 1971 riot. I have been interviewed several times in recent months.

Should the pandemic allow, we in the Forgotten Victims of Attica hope for a memorial on the prison grounds on September 13, 2021, that ensures the riot—in all of its tragedy and sorrow and death—will not be forgotten. And we will solemnly and prayerfully and lovingly remember those we lost.

The fiftieth anniversary would be a significant and meaningful time for the New York governor to join us and to apologize. There is always healing within an apology—even fifty years later.

It is never too late.

Epilogue

In November 2002 I wrote to Corrections Commissioner Glenn Goord letting him know that my mother had just undergone surgery for a cancer that had reemerged.

"I write to you today out of extreme desperation," my letter read. "I ask you, as best you can, to expedite this process and come to a fair and meaningful resolution as soon as possible. My mother and the remaining widows deserve resolution. I can't bear to think that those that would benefit most from your resolutions may not be around by the time all is said and done."

When I wrote that letter, nine widows were alive. By the time the Forgotten Victims received its $12 million award, two of those nine had died.

Our daughter, Aubrey, who was only nine when I wrote to Goord, wanted to contribute.

On a separate piece of paper, in the unmistakable penmanship of an elementary student, she wrote, "I think that my mom's group the Forgotten Victims of Attica is very important to me because my own grandfather was killed in this terrible event in 1971. The group has helped a lot of other people, not just including my family, who have lost loved ones in that time. My grandmother was a widow and she deserves money from the state."

I had not encouraged Aubrey to write the letter. She had just grown up knowing of my quest. It became part of her, just as it did with our youngest daughter, Cassidy.

Epilogue

It's heartbreaking in some ways but also affirming. Both of our children have turned out to be tremendous advocates for themselves, and I think part of that is because they witnessed my many years of working to decipher my history and the history of Attica. They were always there firsthand, sitting in my office as I spoke with state officials and lawmakers. Sometimes those telephone conversations were calm, and sometimes not so calm.

When our daughters saw area code 518—the Albany area code—pop up on our telephone, they would often rush to answer in hopes it was our lobbyist Artie Malkin. They loved to speak with him, and vice versa. They'd then yell to me, "Mom, it's Artie Malkin," trying to mimic his Long Island accent.

We speak about Attica in my home; both daughters have written papers for school about the riot, just as I did. And Aubrey and Cassidy especially know of my father. Our daughters call him "Grandpa Billy." They know of his life and of his death. They know he was a man of service, and that thread has continued within our family. Aubrey is now a nurse practitioner hospitalist in palliative care and Cassidy is a medical laboratory scientist.

Cassidy, the artist in our family, once drew a compelling picture of an Attica prison tower and a separate piece of artwork of the large keys carried by my father at Attica to lock and unlock internal gates. He was carrying the keys at the time of the riot. In her drawing, the three keys are set against a gray backdrop, representing the walls of Attica. A dragonfly sits upon one of the keys, a symbol of transformation and adaptability. The dragonfly, as Cassidy explained to me, appears in people's lives to remind them to embrace lightness and joy, even in difficult times. Throughout her life, Cassidy has believed that every dragonfly that she has seen or that has landed upon her was sent by Grandpa Billy, letting her know he was with her.

Epilogue

Grandpa's Keys by Cassidy Quinn Miller (charcoal on paper). This drawing depicts three keys to the Attica State Correctional Facility. The keys were recovered on the belt of Corrections Officer William Quinn, who was killed in the line of duty during the initial uprising at Attica in September 1971. The keys were one of the few tangible connections to the uprising available to Officer Quinn's family. Drawn by his granddaughter, the gray cement background represents the outside walls of Attica Prison. The dragonfly symbolizes transformation and adaptability. It appears in people's lives to remind them to embrace lightness and joy.

Cassidy's Attica art is so moving that the State Museum plans to use it as part of a mobile exhibit, which will precede the coming larger fixed museum exhibit that was delayed in 2021 by COVID-19.

Our daughters have met so many people of strength and resilience— people like Michael and Sharon Smith, and Malcolm and Nancy Bell, who have stayed at our home many times—and I know they have learned from them, as well. Once, after a memorial service, we were having cake at the QWL, and Aubrey, who is not a fan of icing, was trimming it from her slice. She got a little too aggressive with her icing removal and accidentally flung it across the table, smack onto Malcolm's sweater. Malcolm being Malcolm laughed uproariously and said, "It's good I like icing!"

It's moments like that which remind me that those I've met on my journey, through FVOA and elsewhere, have become like family. There has been pain but there has also been solace and camaraderie and even, as with the flying icing, occasional fun.

Michael, Gary, and I took many trips together to Albany, with Michael typically driving in his massive pickup truck which had a small seating compartment behind the front seat. Gary would sometimes take that seat, because I get car sick, and he would grumble after a few hours because he was then a smoker and was going much longer than he preferred without nicotine. He also would complain of losing feeling in his lower extremities. Gary is not a small man, but he was a good sport—most of the time.

I'll never forget some of those trips, such as when I started from the outset complaining that I'd forgotten my hairdryer, and we were staying overnight at a hotel that I'd learned did not provide one. Apparently, I complained a little too much. Michael finally pulled off the Thruway, paid the toll, then drove over a berm into the parking lot of a Walmart he'd spotted. "Go get your fuckin' hairdryer," he told me. So, I did.

Once, at a dinner before a showing of the Attica documentary from Christine Christopher and David Marshall, a Black man in a jacket with a Black Panthers insignia joined us. Aubrey did not know the history of the organization, and I explained some of it to her later. I'm not sure how much she absorbed, but to this day she speaks of how cool it was to have dinner at the same table with a Black Panther.

I have come so far from the nervous and uncertain woman who was unsure whether she even wanted to show up at the initial meetings of what would become the Forgotten Victims of Attica, the woman with the frequent stomach pains and anxiety. And that road has not only bolstered my confidence but helped me evolve in other ways, again despite the pain.

Twenty years ago, Attica scared me. Attica made me anxious. Attica gave me depression. Anything to do with Attica was like a boogie man.

I remember years ago hearing from Dale Volker that John Hill might be visiting the western New York area. During that time, a Native American man came to my door. I refused to answer, scared that it might be John Hill, the man I was sure had murdered my dad. I then carried a fear of him, and of Attica. I have long since purged all of those fears.

Once in my life I would never have imagined meeting individuals like Richard X. Clark or Frank "Big Black" Smith, much less befriending them. But I did, and my life is better because of it. Yes, they were parts of the puzzle that I was working so hard to arrange, but they also became much more than that. They had suffered, just as those in Forgotten Victims had, and I could not consider them villains as I once did. We shared a pain and experience that others didn't, but we also shared a humanity. I saw it in Richard's eyes and heard it in Richard's words as we sat in that Harlem restaurant so long ago as he explained trying to save the life of my father. I heard it in the many phone calls with Frank, especially in those times when he and I would just pause and sob together, our own union of tears as we realized how alike "Big Black" and "Little White" were.

In some ways, the timing was likely perfect for me to meet former inmates like Frank and Richard. I'm not sure if years before they would have wanted to meet a prison guard's daughter or if I would have felt comfortable meeting them. I don't know if it could have happened any sooner; it was almost like divine timing.

Richard and Frank are now gone, as is Jonathan. I've lost so many during these years. Even in the months of writing this book, I lost my uncle Dean, who had survived as a hostage at Attica, and my uncle Bob, who had worked at the prison and had been off when the riot erupted then was called back to work. Both died from COVID complications, a tragic reminder of the reach of the pandemic we are presently enduring. Both survived Attica but did not survive COVID-19.

In the days before his death, I again talked to uncle Bob about Attica. He did not like to remember the riot, but he would answer questions if I asked him. Our family had long thought that my grandfather on my father's side, who'd been a meat cutter at the prison, had been saved by prisoners who'd secreted him out on a metal cart used within the facility to move large slabs of meat. As we'd heard, they'd covered him up and gotten him out. Somehow this story survived for years. My grandfather, who was so devastated by the loss of my father that he never spoke of the uprising, never affirmed or denied it. I'm not sure if we ever even spoke with him about it, so the story lingered.

But when I spoke to uncle Bob, he remembered that, after he reached the prison on September 9, 1971, to return to work, he saw from the catwalk my grandfather leaving through a gate. Uncle Bob was also sure that prisoners had helped my grandfather hide until he could safely get out, but Bob also said the story about the car was probably false. This story had somehow existed within our family for fifty years, yet it may have been untrue. It just shows how we so rarely discussed Attica within our family and also how there was still so much unknown about the uprising, not only with our familial stories but also with the vast and tragic history.

Malcolm Bell tells me that my father would be proud of me, and I'd like to think that as well. I feel like I'm much closer to him. I think I have a greater knowledge of who he was, and that gives me great peace.

Is that closure? No. I don't think there is closure with Attica. I'm not settled with Attica. I don't think I can ever settle with Attica. It lives within me.

Liz Fink, the lawyer for the Attica inmates, once said, "Justice is what everyone wants, but no one gets." I think I live by Liz's sentence, for what is justice? Is it empirical or something different to each and every one?

I do think FVOA achieved some semblance of justice. A small group of people came together on behalf of our loved ones, and we changed the history of Attica. That is my favorite achievement. Success is so hard to define in these circumstances, for what is the worth of a life left unlived? Or injuries so egregious that you never again are yourself? Or families dismantled? The pain of Attica lives on forever, for those known to us and for many who are not. We will no longer be forgotten because we refused to be.

Even if the final Forgotten Victims of Attica demands are met—records are unsealed in some fashion and the state apologizes—that will not be the end. I'll be watching the State Museum closely to make sure its exhibit remembers the uprising in a balanced way that does justice to its history. Attica is not often equated with justice, but we must not forget it. We need to remember those awful days in a way that ensures we do not make the same mistakes again.

If we do that, then maybe others will not lose fathers, and maybe odysseys like mine won't be necessary. Then men like my father will safely return home from work and live to see their children and grandchildren.

So much of the legacy of Attica is anguish and hurt. I have lived it; it once nearly crippled me emotionally. A half century has passed since the uprising, since that day when the prison whistle would not stop blaring and I was pulled from my classroom and taken to my grandparents' home.

I would not see my father again. But now, I feel as if I know him, truly know him. It has not been easy to reach this point, but I have no regrets. We changed the history of Attica and that journey has profoundly changed me and how I see the world. That is my personal legacy of Attica.

And Malcom . . . I do believe my father would be proud.

Acknowledgments

FROM DEANNE QUINN MILLER

This book started out as a conversation I had with Gary Craig more than ten years ago, but it wasn't until now that I was really ready to talk about my life. Attica will forever be a part of me, but I no longer hate that; I've actually come to love it and embrace it. My journey wasn't easy, and I didn't always know where it was going to take me, but I had faith that I was being guided from above. I've been blessed to have had the opportunity to meet individuals that helped me put my pieces together, lifted me when I felt down, and celebrated with me when I discovered another piece.

Thank you to our agent, Rob Wilson and Diversion Books for taking a chance on me and my story. Thank you, Keith Wallman and staff, for your excellent editing and continued support thorough the process.

To my Attica family, where would I be without you? Gary Horton, Mark and Laurie Cunningham, Mike and Sharon Smith, John and Mary Stockholm, Kentt and Carol Monteleone, Rick and Mary Harcrow, Malcolm and Nancy Bell, Joe Green, Mike Jimenez, Carl Canterbury, Royal Morgan, Brad Lichtenstein, Ray Scott, Arthur Eve, Frank Randazzo, Sister Roz, Jeffrion Aubry, Anthony Annucci, and to everyone in the FVOA, thank you! For those I've missed, I'm sorry!

To those who have passed, that left such an indelible imprint on my life: Jonathan Gradess, Uncle Bob and Aunt Fran Diemoz, Uncle Dean Wright, Frank "Big Black" Smith, G. B. Smith, Richard X. Clark, Liz

Acknowledgments

Fink, Don Jelinek, Grant Marin, Lance Corcoran, and Judge Telesca. For the other ten hostages, whose names I've memorized since I was a little girl; Edward Cunningham, John D'Arcangelo, Elmer Hardie, Herbert Jones, Richard Lewis, John Monteleone, Carl Valone, Elon Werner, Ronald Werner, Harrison Whalen, and other Attica survivors who have since passed. May you all rest in peace.

I'm so thankful for filmmaker Chris Christopher and Attica Historian Heather Ann Thompson, my "go-to girls" who are always at the other end of the phone anytime I'm falling apart or need to complain. I love you both.

To my editor Gary Craig and his lovely wife Charlotte (who was a silent co-editor), thank you for helping me express myself and having confidence in me when I wasn't confident in myself. Thanks for not quitting on me!

To my work family at New York State Defenders Association Veterans Defense Program, for allowing me to take time away to write this book. Special thanks to Gary Horton, Director (yes, we are still working together!), Executive Director Susan Bryant, Executive Assistant Diane DuBois, and the VDP staff.

Thank you, Mom, for answering such difficult questions, fifty years later. I know it wasn't easy for you. Thank you to my sisters Christine, Amy, and Rhoda. Special thanks to the Willard, Diemoz, Miller, and Ferraro families for supporting me all these years.

Most importantly, I thank God for my amazing husband David (often referred to as Saint David) and my beautiful, intelligent, independent girls Aubrey Quinn Wolfe (and my son-in-law Ryan Wolfe) and Cassidy Quinn Miller. You are my whole world, and I hope I made you proud.

Acknowledgments

FROM GARY CRAIG

There are many people whose lives were shattered by the Attica uprising, yet were willing to speak with me over the past twenty years about those painful days and their aftermath. Many of them appear in this book, and I would like to thank them for their strength to remind the world that we should not forget Attica and instead should learn from it. In particular, I would like to thank Michael Smith, who numerous times visited a class I teach at the Rochester Institute of Technology, and his wonderful wife, Sharon, and Minister Raymond Scott, an observer who also has been open with his time and memories, as difficult as they can be.

There are others who, like me, became intertwined with the history of Attica in different ways, and they have helped tremendously with this book. Local filmmaker and friend Christine Christopher has been immensely supportive of our work, as has Heather Ann Thompson, whose *Blood in the Water: The Attica Prison Uprising of 1971 and Its Legacy*, is the authoritative Attica history. Thanks also to Gary Horton, whose work on behalf of the Forgotten Victims of Attica cannot be overstated, and to filmmaker Brad Lichtenstein, who shared his time and memories from his investigative work with the Attica riot. And a special thanks to former Attica prosecutor Malcolm Bell, whose foreword graces this book and whose gratis editing was just one of so many indications of his boundless kindness.

I would be remiss if I didn't mention two people who are no longer with us—Frank "Big Black" Smith, whose spirit and courage were unmatched, and US District Judge Michael Telesca, with whom I often spoke about Attica and who held the Constitution dear. I hope this book captures their character.

Thanks to our agent—Rob Wilson—and to Keith Wallman and his team at Diversion Books for their willing support and help with this project.

Acknowledgments

Thanks also to my editors at the *Democrat and Chronicle*—Matthew Leonard, Michael Kilian, Scott Norris—who allowed me time away from work for this book.

I am blessed with two wonderful daughters, Brittany and Aileen, and am married to my best friend, Charlotte. They have always been my biggest supporters. I cannot thank them enough.

Mostly, I need to thank Dee Quinn Miller: As this book recounts, we met more than twenty years ago, brought together by Attica. I have always found her life journey inspiring, a tale of reconciliation and resilience that can be a lesson for us all, especially at times like the present. I am touched and honored that Dee, who has become a dear friend, allowed me to help tell her story, and I hope more than anything that I have done it a fraction of the justice it deserves. As a society, we too often build walls—based on race or income level or ethnicity or gender or religion—and allow ourselves to be exploited by those who try to keep those walls in place. Dee could have spent a life boxed in by those walls. Instead, she leveled them. Let us learn from her and maybe we all can do the same.

Sources

T his book is largely constructed from my memories and records from my years with Forgotten Victims of Attica. Others, as co-author Gary Craig and I note in our acknowledgements, also helped fill in some gaps. And there are still others whose names appear throughout this book whom we reached out to for confirmation of details large and small.

There are two books that were vital resources for some of the history we recount. While, as we note here, there were articles and research and films that we used once or occasionally, these books provided us with essential historical background. They are *Blood in the Water: The Attica Prison Uprising of 1971 and Its Legacy* by Heather Ann Thompson and *The Turkey Shoot: Tracking the Attica Cover-Up* by Malcolm Bell. Also particularly valuable were Tom Wicker's *A Time to Die: The Attica Prison Revolt*; Richard X. Clark's *The Brothers of Attica*; and *Attica Justice* by Don Jelinek.

Though, as we now know, there are portions of *The Official Report of the New York State Special Commission on Attica*, also known as *The McKay Report*, that can be challenged through the lens of history, we also utilized the commission's report for our research.

Two films also provided details for our research. They are *Ghosts of Attica*, from Icarus Films and Brad Lichtenstein, and *Criminal Injustice: Death and Politics at Attica*, from Blue Sky Project and Christine Christopher and David Marshall.

Sources

The transcripts from Attica inmate testimony in federal court in Rochester in 2000 and from the Forgotten Victims of Attica in Albany and Rochester in 2002 were also essential to our research.

Gary Craig has written dozens of stories since 2000 about Attica, the inmate settlement, and the Forgotten Victims of Attica. While not cited in the chapter-by-chapter sourcing that follows, those stories and his records were used throughout this book for background.

For our research we also turned to the following sources:

CHAPTER ONE

"Riots and Reconstruction," Cayuga Museum of History and Art.

Lawrence Van Gelder, "Prison Has History of Riot and Reform," *New York Times*, Nov. 5, 1970.

"Attica Correctional Facility," New York State Archives, Cultural Education Center.

"Evolution of New York State's Prison System," Corrections History, New York Society.

"Willie Sutton," FBI History.

Michael Beebe and Dan Herbeck, "Attica Still Inspires Terror in Those Behind Its Walls," *The Buffalo News*, Sept. 9, 1996.

CHAPTER THREE

Andrew L. Yarrow, "Reporter's Notebook: After 17 Years, The Attica Trial Lives," *New York Times*, Jan. 11, 1992.

"Jack Katz," Peoplepill.com, Wikipedia.org.

Robert D. McFadden, "Ex-Attica Inmate Wins $4 Million for Reprisals After '71 Uprising," *New York Times*, June 6, 1997.

www.archives.nysed.gov/research/oag/attica-timeline.

Sources

Maggie Haberman, "Brutal Attica Chapter Finally Ends," *New York Post*, Jan. 7, 2000.

CHAPTER FOUR

Transcripts, WBTA Radio Show.

CHAPTER FIVE

Laurel Auchampaugh, "An Attica hostage's true story," *The Auburn Citizen*, May 26, 2019.

"Gustafsen Lake," www.indigenousfoundations.arts.ubc.ca /gustafsen_lake/.

CHAPTER SIX

Mallory Diefenback, "Honoring the Fallen," *The (Batavia) Daily News*, Sept. 14, 2016.

CHAPTER SEVEN

Jonathan Gradess and Gary Horton, "It's Up to Cuomo to Apologize for Attica," (*Albany*) *Times-Union*, Oct. 4. 2011.

CHAPTER EIGHT

"Widows, Children of Slain Attica Guards Seek Aid, an Apology," The Associated Press, May 24, 2000.

David Montgomery, "Essentially Arthur Eve Has Turned His Life into a Crusade," *The Buffalo News*, Nov. 15, 1992.

"Arthur Eve Honored on Retirement," WBFO.

CHAPTER ELEVEN

Douglas Martin, "Frank Smith, 71, Is Dead; Sought Justice After Attica," *New York Times*, Aug. 3, 2004.

Sources

CHAPTER THIRTEEN

Tom Wicker, "Death of a Brother," *New York Times*, Aug. 24, 1971.

Kevin Kelley, "Wicker's Word," *Seven Days*, Jan. 9. 2002.

Adam Gopnik, "Learning from the Slaughter in Attica," *New Yorker*, Aug. 22, 2016.

CHAPTER FOURTEEN

Tom Wicker, "Attica's Forgotten Victims," *New York Times*, Sept. 23, 2000.

CHAPTER FIFTEEN

Joseph Lelyveld, "First of Attica Uprising Leaders is Released, but He Fears Arrest at Any Time," *New York Times,* Feb. 9, 1972.

"Attica Brother Richard X. Clark and Danny Myers Talk," YouTube. com, Nov. 21, 2013.

CHAPTER SEVENTEEN

Dale Anderson, "Eugene C. Tenney, Personal Injury Trial Lawyer, Represented Attica Hostage Families," *The Buffalo News*, Nov. 5, 2019.

CHAPTER EIGHTEEN

Jennifer Gonnerman, "Remembering Attica," *The Village Voice*, Sept. 4, 2001.

"Vigil to Mark Attica Riot," Associated Press, Sept. 3, 2001.

Wunderground.com, weather history, Sept. 11, 2001.

"World Trade Center Cases in the New York Workers' Compensation System," New York State Workers' Compensation Board, Sept. 2009.

Sources

"Looking Back: The Attica Uprising and Aftermath," YouTube.com, June 7, 2013.

CHAPTER TWENTY-THREE

Sam Roberts, "Donald Jelinek, Lawyer for Attica Prisoners, Dies at 82," *New York Times*, July 3, 2016.

"Scott Christianson biography," New York State Writers Institute, State University of New York.

CHAPTER TWENTY-FOUR

Jeffrey Schmalz, "Lobbyist Tips on Getting Their Way," *New York Times*, Aug. 12, 1985.

CHAPTER TWENTY-FIVE

Robert Hanley, "Guard Who Lied About Attica May Be Disciplined by State," *New York Times*, March 21, 1975.

Dedicated to Justice: Honorable Michael A. Telesca, Northlight Productions and producer Matthew Spaull, 2015

CHAPTER TWENTY-SIX

Sam Roberts, "New York is Cataloging, and Returning, Bloody Relics of 1971 Attica Assault," *New York Times*, Oct. 5, 2014.

CHAPTER TWENTY-EIGHT

Sam Roberts, "Jonathan Gradess, Legal Defender of the Poor, Dies at 72," *New York Times*, Oct. 31, 2019.

Jonathan Gradess and Gary Horton, "It's Up to Cuomo to Apologize for Attica," *Times-Union*, Oct. 4. 2011.

Lesa Quayle Ferguson, "A Haunted Walk in Perrysburg," *Buffalo Vibe*, Oct. 19, 2016.

Sources

Adam Gopnik, "Learning from the Slaughter in Attica," *The New Yorker*, Aug. 22, 2016.

Robert Hanley, "Guard Who Lied About Attica May Be Disciplined by State," *New York Times*, March 21, 1975.

ww3.nysif.com › media › Files › PDF › ONLINE_PUBS.

William Glaberson, "Echoes of Violence: Attica's Story Retold in Court," *New York Times*, Dec. 10, 1991.

Index

Index

Index

Index

Index

Index

Index

About the Authors

Deanne Quinn Miller is cofounder of the Forgotten Victims of Attica and the daughter of Correctional Officer William Quinn, the first casualty of the Attica Prison Riot. With Miller's leadership, the Forgotten Victims secured $12 million in reparations for its members, counseling for all who sought it, and an annual memorial at the prison. The organization continues to push for other goals—the unsealing of the remaining thousands of pages of nonpublic riot records and an apology from the New York State.

Miller has previously worked as the executive director of the Genesee Veterans Support Network and received the state Women Veterans in the Justice System award in 2016 and the Women of Distinction Award in 2017 for her work with veterans. She graduated cum laude from the University of New York at Buffalo with a BS in Consumer and Family Studies. Since 2014, she has been the program coordinator for the Veterans Defense Program of the New York State Defenders Association, a program that provides support and legal aid to struggling veterans who become involved in the criminal justice system. Miller lives in Batavia, New York, and is married with two daughters.

Gary Craig is an investigative reporter with the Rochester *Democrat and Chronicle*. He has won national awards for his reporting and writing—including multiple awards for reporting on prison conditions—and more than two dozen state, regional, and national honors. He is the author of *Seven Million: A Cop, a Priest, a Soldier for the IRA, and the Still-Unsolved Rochester Brink's Heist.*

Craig covered the resolution of the decades-long lawsuit filed by Attica inmates against the state. Since 2000, he has written extensively about Attica, reporting on the birth and work of the Forgotten Victims of Attica, and the efforts to open Attica records. Craig lives in Rochester, New York, and is married with two daughters.